UNSHAKEABLE

THE LIFE OF A TRUE JESUS FOLLOWER

By Daniel Aguilar

Unshakeable: The Life of a True Jesus Follower

Trilogy Christian Publishers A Wholly Owned Subsidary of Trinity Broadcasting Network

2442 Michelle Drive Tustin, CA 92780

Rights Department, 2442 Michelle Drive, Tustin, CA 92780.

Trilogy Christian Publishing/TBN and colophon are trademarks of Trinity Broadcasting Network.

For information about special discounts for bulk purchases, please contact Trilogy Christian Publishing.

Trilogy Disclaimer: The views and content expressed in this book are those of the author and may not necessarily reflect the views and doctrine of Trilogy Christian Publishing or the Trinity Broadcasting Network.

Manufactured in the United States of America

10 9 8 7 6 5 4 3 2 1

Library of Congress Cataloging-in-Publication Data is available.

ISBN: 978-1-68556-338-7

E-ISBN: 978-1-68556-339-4

DEDICATION

I dedicate this book to my boys, Joseph and Elisha. The
LORD has worked through them to show me
the full truth of the Gospel.

ACKNOWLEDGMENTS

I would like to thank:

My friend Jordan, for encouraging me to finish this book.

My friend Lisa, for being the first person to review and read this book.

My wife's family, who prayed for me to publish this book.

My mom and brother, who shared encouraging words with me throughout my writing process.

My beautiful wife, Sonja, for reading my book and agreeing with me to see it published.

The LORD God Himself, for providing me the opportunity to give Him all the glory!

INTRODUCTION

Therefore, when we could no longer endure it, we thought it good to be left in Athens alone, and sent Timothy, our brother and minister of God, and our fellow laborer in the gospel of Christ, to establish you and encourage you concerning your faith, that no one should be shaken by these afflictions; for you yourselves know that we are appointed to this. For, in fact, we told you before when we were with you that we would suffer tribulation, just as it happened, and you know. For this reason, when I could no longer endure it, I sent to know your faith, lest by some means the tempter had tempted you, and our labor might be in vain.

1 Thessalonians 3:1–5

Only knowing the blessings makes you breakable but having awareness of afflictions makes you unshakeable!

It was 2 a.m., and I was sitting on my mattress in my bedroom. I was struggling whether to wholeheartedly follow Jesus or not. I was afraid of starting to walk with Him and then giving up halfway. I was scared that this new life with Jesus would become too hard, I would quit, and then people would say, "See, there is no God. Daniel couldn't do it, so there must not be a God." So, at that time in my life, I asked God this question, "How do I know that everything is going to work out if I give my life to You?" I had a little TV in my room, and I would usually leave the TV on for white noise in the background. I did so on this late night/ early morning while I was praying to God. God answered

7

my question through one of those TV shows. My TV only received two channels. I had basic shows to watch like *The King of Queens, Frasier,* and my favorite, *Late Night Texas Hold 'em.* After *Texas Hold 'em*, the TV show *Scrubs* would come on. The setting of the show was in a hospital, and it had a mixture of comical and serious moments throughout. Once *Texas Hold 'em* was over, as soon as I asked God that question, I heard one of the Scrubs characters reference a Bible verse to one of the other characters. I am not making this up. One of the nurses on the show (Laverne) played the character of a Christian woman with a strong faith in God. At the end of this specific episode ("My No-Good Reason," Season 6: Episode 14), a patient died, and Laverne comforted one of the doctors by saying that "God works all things for good," and then she referenced Romans 8:28. Once I heard her say Romans 8:28, I grabbed my Bible, looked in the table of contents, found the page number to Romans 8, looked at verse 28, and it read, *"And we know that all things work together for good to those who love God, to those who are the called according to His purpose."* God answered me! I asked Him, "How do I know that it is all going to work out?" He promised through His Word and by His Holy Spirit that it would all work out in the end!

All Things Work Together for Good

I can say without a shadow of a doubt that God has kept this promise to me. After saying yes to follow Jesus with all my heart, God has done many extraordinary things in my life. He took me out of my old life that consisted of drug addiction and sexual sin. He healed my broken heart from bad relationships with past girlfriends and family. He called me to be a pastor and sent me to Multnomah University (formerly known as Multnomah Bible College) to train me up. He gave me the opportunity to play two years of college basketball at Multnomah University as well. God led me to my home church at East River Fellowship, where I have had the privilege to do the following: Be the youth pastor, young adults' pastor, men's pastor, associate pastor, preach in the main service, teach discipleship classes, go on five missions' trips to Haiti and Mexico, see people give their lives to Jesus, and much more! What I am most grateful for is that I met my wife at East River. We have been married since March 5, 2016, and we have two beautiful boys together, Joseph (who is in heaven) and Elisha. I say all this to brag on the goodness of God (Romans 2:4)![1] God loves us so much (1 John 4:19, John 3:16). As the good Father He is, He wants the very best for us (Jeremiah 29:11). I have been following Jesus since February 4, 2011, and He has provided for me in every way. God has promised that with Him, all things will work together for good, and I will make it to the very end (Philippians 1:6). This applies to you as well!

The Suffering Saint

However, there is more to following Jesus than I realized. I did not realize that a little over two years after saying yes to Jesus, I would begin to encounter many unexpected trials, so much hardship, that it made me question my faith in God. It made me wonder if He was even real. *Why isn't He stopping this? Is He the one initiating it? Does He care about my pain? How long must I endure this?* I had many questions about my faith walk with Jesus as I began to encounter trials. Between August 2013 and August 2020, I went through many intense hardships. During that season, it was not pleasant. I didn't agree with it. If I had the choice, I would have avoided it. But I had the choice to either stay with God or stray from God. Instead of giving up, the Holy Spirit helped me, and I chose to trust God, to trust that He knows what He is doing (Proverbs 3:5–6). I can honestly say that after those seven years of consistent hardship, that God is more than faithful (2 Thessalonians 3:3; 2 Timothy 2:13)! Look at the verses following the promise I received from Romans 8:28.

> *For whom He foreknew, He also predestined to be conformed to the image of His Son, that He might be the firstborn among many brethren. Moreover whom He predestined, these He also called; whom He called, these He also justified; and whom He justified, these He also glorified.*

Romans 8:29–30

What stands out to me is the part where it says, *"to be conformed to the image of His Son."*[2] That word conformed means: of the same shape as, similar in form, and like-natured. As followers of Jesus, we are called to be like Jesus (1 John 2:6; 1 Corinthians 11:1; Ephesians 5:1–2). Jesus had to go through suffering to become the Savior, the Person that He was ultimately meant to be. When I received the promise that God would work all things for good, I only received part of the story. A simple tool the Holy Spirit gave me one day regarding reading the Bible was, "Keep reading." If I had continued reading the verses that followed that promise, I would have seen that not only does blessing lay ahead of me, but so does hardship. Following Jesus doesn't guarantee us a life without hardship, as many people believe. Following Jesus guarantees that we will have hardship (Matthew 7:14).

But God promises that He will be with us through it all. He will strengthen us. He will provide for us and prepare us.

Only knowing the blessings makes you breakable but having awareness of afflictions makes you unshakeable!

Why Suffering?

This is where I see most people lose their faith in God. They can't understand how a good God can allow suffering in their life. It's because they don't understand the purpose behind trials/hardships. God wants us to become like Jesus. Because when people see Jesus, they see the Father (John 14:9). When people see the Father, they see God. When people see God, they see the truth in this life and have the chance to spend the rest of eternity with Him (John 17:3). When people see us, they should see God in us (Ephesians 5:1). This means that people will see Jesus in us, and then our lives will point people to Father God so they can follow Him too (Galatians 2:20)! Genesis 1:26–27 says that God made us in His image. We resemble Him like children do their parents. But because of the fallen state of this world (Genesis 3), we are so far off from our original image. This means that God will use hardships to mold us into the character and person of Jesus. We just read that in Romans 8:29, *"For whom He foreknew, He also predestined to be conformed to the image of His Son, that He might be the firstborn among many brethren."*

The Suffering Savior

Jesus went through much hardship. We can see that throughout the Gospels. Even the apostles and disciples that followed in His footsteps went through trials as well.

> *Who, in the days of His flesh, when He had offered up prayers and supplications, with vehement cries and tears to Him who was able to save Him from death, and was heard because of His godly fear, though He was a Son, yet He learned obedience by the things which He suffered. And having been perfected, He became the author of eternal salvation to all who obey Him.*

Hebrews 5:7–9

Jesus' journey was not complete until He endured the stage in His life of suffering. This part of Hebrews is referencing Jesus in the Garden of Gethsemane in Matthew 26. Jesus had obeyed His Father all the way up to this point, and then He was tempted to possibly not obey Him. He cries out three different times in Matthew 26 to see if there is any other possible way for Him to be the Savior of the world without having to go through suffering. He had to endure betrayal, false accusations, beatings, scourging, being spit on, being lied about, ridiculed, mocking, hung on a cross, and then death.

But in the same passage, He also said three different times, "Not my will, but Your will be done." Jesus endured suffering to become the Savior. Jesus had human fears and doubts just like us, but He had a stronger desire to set aside His personal feelings and to follow God's will for His life. *"Looking unto Jesus, the author and finisher of our faith, who for the joy that was set before Him endured the cross, despising the shame, and has sat down at the right hand of the throne of God"* (Hebrews 12:2). Jesus had to endure suffering to become who He was meant to be and so will you. *"For to this you were called, because Christ also suffered for us, leaving us an example, that you should follow His steps"* (1 Peter 2:21).

The Full Story

This book is not all about suffering. It is about God being faithful to fulfill His promises in your life, regardless of what obstacles come your way. My intention in writing this book is for you to have the full story of what being a Jesus follower truly looks like. I want you to see the blessed life of being a Jesus follower. Yet, I do not want you to give up on your walk with God because you become blindsided by trials. I want to share the whole counsel of God with you (Acts 20:27). Following Jesus is the best decision you will ever make in your life. But you have to know the full truth, that it won't be full of sunshine and rainbows all the time. I wish I knew back then, what I know now, that trials and hardships are part of the life of a true Jesus follower. They cannot be avoided, but they can be endured, and they are for a purpose (James 1:2–4).

My hope for you in reading this book comes from the opening verses in 1 Thessalonians 3:1–5. I am acting as Timothy in writing this book. I hope that you will be established and encouraged in your faith. That you will be unshakeable in your faith in The LORD God. That suffering will not make you stray from God; rather, in suffering, you will stay with God. That the enemy would not tempt you to walk away from God; because you are now aware that not only is blessing part of being a Jesus follower, but suffering is also part of following Him too.

Joseph in Genesis

There is no better example to look at than that of Joseph in the Book of Genesis 37–50. Joseph went through much hardship, but he was also blessed beyond his imagination. Regardless of the ups and downs in his life, he continued to walk with God until the day he died. We will see the hopes and dreams given to him, the hardships he endured, and the outcome of his life that saved an entire nation, the very nation that our Lord and Savior Jesus Christ came through. Joseph foreshadows Jesus. The things Joseph went through represent what Jesus would go through for us. Joseph's life is meant to point us to Christ! Therefore, throughout this character/story, we can see the life of a true Jesus follower!

Joseph's Journey

Difficult family situation Hated by his brothers Brothers plotted his death Cast into a pit	Sold into slavery Away from home Accused of Rape/Adultery	Put in prison (a dungeon) Forgotten in prison	Away from family Emotional distress with family	Tough life
Was loved Chosen Had a God dream Protected	**God was with him Faithful Successful Served Given authority 2nd in command Blessed**	**God was with him Mercy Favor Prospered Authority Wisdom Interpreted dreams**	**God raised him to power 2nd in command to Pharaoh Saw his family again Had God's heart Provider Had his own family**	**God life**

I broke this lengthy story down into three simple movements: *the beginning, the testing, and the healing.* The nine chapters within lay out the storyline of the life of a true Jesus follower from beginning to end.

Chapter One—God had a plan for your life before you were even born. Your family background does not determine your future.

Chapter Two—God has given you a specific calling/vision for your life. It gives Him glory, points others to Him, and gives you fulfillment as you walk in what you were created to do.

Chapter Three—It will cost you everything to fulfill what He called you to do. You can't hold anything back.

Chapter Four—The LORD is always with you. He paid a great price to be close to you. Hardships will not dismiss His presence from you.

Chapter Five—Temptation will come at you, but in Jesus, you can overcome it. You can live free.

Chapter Six—God has given you spiritual gifts. Just like your calling, it's for God first, others second, and you last. But it's amazing to have Him work through you in miraculous ways.

Chapter Seven—You have a choice to live His way or your way. His way is difficult, but His way is better. We have to trust Him and do things His way.

Chapter Eight—You are set apart by God. You are not like everyone else. As you die to yourself, others will find life in Jesus. It is a great cost to you, but a great deal for others.

Chapter Nine—God is good no matter what. He is so good that He told us the truth upfront. He had it written down in His Word so that we would not be caught off guard. God is not the problem; our ignorance of His truth is. He has told us the truth. We can trust Him for who He is.

Personal or Small Group Questions—There is also a compilation of questions derived from each chapter in this book. You can choose to answer them personally or in a small group. You can answer the questions after you read each chapter, each section, or you can read the entire book and answer the questions afterward.

I will let the Scriptures speak for themselves and reveal to us what this walk with God truly looks like. I trust the Holy Spirit to bring clarity and hope to the topic of suffering in the life of a Jesus follower while also discovering the blessed aspects of the Christ-centered life. I will be using examples from my personal story as a testimony to the goodness and faithfulness of God (Revelation 12:11). I pray that by the end of this book, that you will establish a greater love and faith towards Jesus. I pray that your life and faith in Jesus will be unshakeable!

Only knowing the blessings makes you breakable but having awareness of afflictions makes you unshakeable!

TABLE OF CONTENTS

PROLOGUE

You will see parts in the book that says, "Please take a moment to read this part of Scripture in your Bible." It is important for the reader to not skip over those Scriptures. They help provide context to the overall flow of the book. Since the book covers such a big portion of Scripture, I found it necessary to not write out big portions of Scripture unless they pertain directly to the account of Joseph in the Book of Genesis. So please have your Bible with you as you read this book. You are going to need it!

THE
BEGINNING

CHAPTER ONE
WE ARE FAMILY

*A true Jesus follower's future is
not determined by their family
background!*

*"Now Jacob dwelt in the land where his father
was a stranger, in the land of Canaan.
This is the history of Jacob."*

Genesis 37:1–2a

Before we talk about Joseph, let's unpack the life of his father, Jacob. I am going to paraphrase this section, but these details can be found in the earlier pages of Genesis. Jacob is the son of Isaac, who is the son of Abraham (Genesis 22). Jacob had a twin brother named Esau, and they did not get along. Jacob set out away from his family to start his own life and came across a beautiful woman named Rachel. He vowed to work seven years for her father to ask his daughter's hand in marriage. Rachel's father, Laban, agreed but ended up tricking Jacob by giving his oldest daughter, Leah, to him. Laban did this because Leah was the oldest sister, and it was not customary to let the younger sister marry before the older. Jacob worked another seven years for Rachel's hand in marriage. After fourteen years of labor, Jacob received Rachel but now had two wives, and they are sisters.

It is worth noting that just because the Bible describes the lives of people, it does not mean that God condones their behavior. Genesis 2:24 reveals God's heart and design for marriage; it is to be between one man and one woman. In ancient culture, men had multiple wives. But God's heart is for men to have one wife. Look at what the Holy Spirit says,

> *This is a faithful saying: If a man desires the position of a bishop, he desires a good work. A bishop then must be blameless, the husband of one wife, temperate, sober-minded, of good behavior, hospitable, able to teach.*

1 Timothy 3:1–2

God also says,

> *Truly, these times of ignorance God overlooked, but now commands all men everywhere to repent, because He has appointed a day on which He will judge the world in righteousness by the Man whom He has ordained. He has given assurance of this to all by raising Him from the dead.*

Acts 17:30–31

I wanted to clarify this because the story of Jacob gets more troubling. Rachel and Leah had multiple feuds with each other about when Jacob would spend time with each of them as their husband. They also had major arguments as to how many children each woman would get from Jacob. Children were the inheritance and heritage of women in the ancient world. Rachel had a maidservant named Bilhah and Leah had a maidservant named Zilpah. The competition between the sisters increased so greatly that they each gave their maidservants to sleep with Jacob so that they could have children, and those children would be accredited to the sisters. I could only imagine the hurt and the pain that took place in each of these women. Women are meant to be cherished and valued. No wife should have to compete for her husband's attention. No woman should be used for the benefit of others. This is not God's way; this is the Bible showing the heart of sinful man. Read Ephesians 5:25–33 to see how husbands and wives are to treat one another. Yet, God is so loving, patient, and faithful that He still works through the fallen state of man to achieve His purpose and our salvation. I will not be writing on Genesis 38, but you can look at Genesis 38 for more illustrations about God working through the fallen state of man for His good.

As a result of the feuds between the sisters, Jacob ends up having thirteen children: twelve sons and one daughter.

> *Now the sons of Jacob were twelve: the sons of Leah were Reuben, Jacob's firstborn, and Simeon, Levi, Judah, Issachar, and Zebulun; the sons of Rachel were Joseph and Benjamin; the sons of Bilhah, Rachel's maidservant, were Dan and Naphtali; and the sons of Zilpah, Leah's maidservant, were Gad and Asher. These were the sons of Jacob who were born to him in Padan Aram.*

Genesis 35:22b–26

Dinah was the name of his only daughter (Genesis 34:1). This means that Joseph had one biological father, one biological mother, one biological brother, three stepmoms, ten half-brothers, and one-half sister. Joseph did not come from a perfect family background.

What Does Your Family Background Look Like?

I remember at the age of seven years old; I was living with my mom, two of my brothers, one of my sisters, and her three children all in one home. My oldest brother and sister were living on their own, and my dad was incarcerated. My mom was the only source of our income. She raised four of her children and three grandchildren on less than $20,000 a year. She often went to our church food pantry, which helped us greatly. There was one week where we could not afford milk. We had to drink powdered milk and mix it with water. One morning all we had was plain cheerios and powdered milk to go with it. My twin brother and I loaded the cereal bowl with sugar, and when we were done, you could see the mountain of sugar protruding through the milk. I also remember a time when my brother and I were looking for money in the couch cushions. We came across what looked like a checkbook. Inside of it contained a $5 food stamp. This was when food stamps were made of paper, not like a food stamp card that people use today. My brother and I were so excited that we went to the local mini-mart and bought $5 worth of candy. Looking back now, I see that we had very little.

It's important to note that Joseph grew up in a dysfunctional home. I have heard many people blame the lack of their success as an adult due to how they were raised. We all have childhood wounds. Some are more significant than others. We all have different challenges that stem from many uncontrollable factors in our lives. We can't help whether we were born male or female, what color we are, whether we are rich or poor, etc. And depending on those factors, the road to success may be more difficult. But regardless of what we were born into or how we were raised, when we encounter God, everything changes!

There Is Hope

At such a young age, I did not have the best odds for success on my side. But God had a plan for my life, and He has a plan for yours too (Jeremiah 29:11)! The LORD moved through people to help me succeed. God moved the hearts of many people to make sure I was taken care of and to make sure that I became the man He made me to be. As I share these personal stories, I want you to think about your own story and how God has provided for you, regardless of your broken home life.

There was a program called "Angel Tree," which helped inmates provide Christmas gifts to their children. I benefited from this ministry as a child, as the gifts would include one set of clothing and one toy each Christmas. Even though I did not spend many Christmas days with my dad, the people who started this program provided an outlet where many children like myself were able to experience a small connection with their fathers, even though their dads were not present in the home. Though I never met the founder (Mary Kay Beard) of Angel Tree Prison Fellowship, I have benefited from her answering the call of God in her life and being the person God made her to be.

My twin brother and I participated in the Royal Rangers ministry at our church. This ministry was founded by Reverend Johnnie Barnes in the Assembly of God Church.

Commander Bacon was our outpost leader, and he had twin boys as well. We befriended them, and this family poured into my brother and me. I remember going to a retreat with our Outpost 255 group. There was an altercation that took place between one of the boys and my brother. I stepped in, confronted the boy, and ended up getting into my first fight. Commander Bacon came into our cabin to see what the commotion was and, with tears in his eyes, said, "What are you guys doing? We don't do that to each other. We are brothers in Christ. You have too much life ahead of you to start this nonsense now. Knock it off and make up. I love you all too much to see you like this." Because of the lack of fatherhood in the lives of most of the kids around me, fighting and drug abuse were common. But I will never forget that moment because Commander Bacon believed in us. He believed that there was more to our lives. He saw something that we didn't. I am forever impacted because of his courage to speak into the lives of those young men in Outpost 255.

My oldest sister and her husband would host family dinners every Sunday, and they made some of the best food. The famous shrimp fettuccine alfredo was an absolute favorite. Having that consistency as a family formed stability in us. Being able to sit at the dinner table together, play in the backyard with our nieces and cousins showed us what a healthy home looked like. Her husband was our football coach in grade school and middle school. He bought us the gear we needed for the football season, and he and another parent sent us to an Oregon State University football camp to sharpen our skills. We would have never been able to afford that camp on our own. This showed my brother and me that we were valuable. There was a time when my brother and I wanted to buy these diamond earrings for my mom for Mother's Day. They were $200, and we were in middle school, and we didn't have jobs to afford them. My sister's husband gave us the $200 for the earrings but then said we could work it off by mowing the back lawn every other week. At $10 for each mow, we worked our way towards paying off that gift. This instilled a greater work ethic in my brother and me. The lessons my sister and her husband taught us and the lessons they modeled for us helped us greatly.

We were also introduced to the Baumgartner family through one of their sons. This son and I were in the same class, and, one day, we were playing football out at recess. My brother and I were the new kids from California, and we beat these kids in a football game. But then this Baumgartner boy challenged me to a basketball game. He beat me badly! Once we got back to class, he began to recruit me and my brother to play basketball for his dad's team. His dad was the elementary school football coach as well. Not only did this family teach us how to play basketball, but they took us under their wings and cared for us. They took us to and from our basketball games. They let us stay over at their homes. They had us over for dinners. They even took us on their family vacations with them. They treated my brother and me like their own children. My brother and I continued playing basketball from 6th grade through our sophomore year of high school. But one of the best moments in my life took place when coach Baumgartner was able to come watch me play in my college basketball game in Portland, Oregon. This family taught us so much more than basketball; they taught us important life lessons.

One more story before I drive the point of this chapter home. My mom had a children's daycare, and through this career, she became friends with one of the mothers. My brother and I were about to graduate 8th grade, and we were required to dress formally for the occasion. We did not own formal dress attire. So, my mom's friend offered to buy what we needed. She bought our dress pants, dress shirt, tie, and shoes. This was a great help. But then she said to us, "I only ask one request of you boys in return. Let me share my story with you." She sat down with us, two thirteen-year-old boys who she saw as future men. She proceeded to tell us a story from her life that I will never forget. I won't go into too much detail, but she told us how she was raped by her boyfriend and his friends. She told us this story so that we would not become men that use women. She saw something better in us and shared her pain so that we would grow up to respect women. That moment defined my brother and me to be different, and that truth steered us in the right direction. Today, my brother and I are both married to women we love and respect. We are both fathers and have found a deeper love for the mothers of our children.

There are so many more people I could mention and thank for helping me become the man I am today. All the sports coaches throughout my life that helped pay for athletic insurance taught us morals and encouraged us. All the childcare sitters that helped my mom watch my brother and me while she worked. Those sitters protected us and provided for us. All the family members in my family and my wife's side of the family that have poured into me spiritually and financially. And all the people at my church, especially my pastor, who continually support me.

God Gets the Final Say

Too often, we let our family dynamics and background determine our future. We look back at our family line, the struggles, the choices made which were out of our control, and then we throw our hands up and say, "Well, this is my life, and there is nothing I can do about it." Wrong! It doesn't matter what type of family background you have. God can work through any situation! Gideon, King David, and King Saul all claimed to be the least within their families and within their family lines. They all came from the tribe of Benjamin, which was considered the least out of the twelve tribes of Israel. Then they were the lowest on the totem pole within their own households. They would consider themselves the lowest of low in all of Israel. And yet, those were the very people that God chose to work through for His purpose and glory!

> *For you see your calling, brethren, that not many wise according to the flesh, not many mighty, not many noble, are called. But God has chosen the foolish things of the world to put to shame the wise, and God has chosen the weak things of the world to put to shame the things which are mighty; and the base things of the world and the things which are despised God has chosen, and the things which are not, to bring to nothing the things that are, that no flesh should glory in His presence. But of Him you are in Christ Jesus, who became for us wisdom from God—and righteousness and sanctification and redemption— that, as it is written, "He who glories, let him glory in the Lord.*

1 Corinthians 1:26–31

Don't let the culture or your family history define you negatively. Let God define you! Let God shape your future! If you come from a broken home, then you are a perfect candidate to partner with God to go and heal others who are broken. Be encouraged. God will work miracles from His own hand, and He will stir the hearts of others to help support you in your life call and purpose!

A true Jesus follower's future is not determined by their family background!

CHAPTER TWO
THE GOD DREAM

A true Jesus follower has a vision for their life!

Our church regularly travels to Haiti to help people. Our mission's pastor's heart was stirred up years ago after the devastating earthquake hit their capital. Once she became part of the leadership in our church, she began to take teams from our church to pour into the lives of the Haitians. There is much hopelessness there. Much pain and turmoil. Most Haitians are barely surviving, and they truly don't know if they are going to be alive tomorrow. But there are those who trust in God, and they know that He provides for them. One Haitian told me, "I haven't eaten in three days, and I don't know where my next meal will come from, but I know God will provide" (Matthew 6:25–34).

As I talked with one of the young pastor's I asked him this question, "What gives you hope to keep moving forward with your life?" He replied in English, "I have a picture in my head." I asked for clarification, and this is what he explained to me. He said, "I don't have much, but I do have a vegetable garden. Every day I take care of my garden because it is the source of my income. This helps me make it. But I have this picture in my head that gives me hope. Something that tells me to keep going. Something that says don't give up." I then realized that he was talking about having a vision for his life. A vision was cast in his heart and mind, which allowed him to keep moving forward during a very difficult life. This vision gave him the drive and purpose to live. That is when I realized it is important that we, too, have a vision for our lives! Proverbs 29:18 (KJV) says, *"Where there is no vision, the people perish: but he that keepeth the law, happy is he."* We need vision, and we need a God dream! This is exactly what we see in Genesis 37 as we dive into the story of Joseph.

> *Joseph, being seventeen years old, was feeding the flock with his brothers. And the lad was with the sons of Bilhah and the sons of Zilpah, his father's wives; and Joseph brought a bad report of them to his father.*
> *Now Israel loved Joseph more than all his children, because he was the son of his old age. Also he made him a tunic of many colors. But when his brothers saw that their father loved him more than all his brothers, they hated him and could not speak peaceably to him.*
> *Now Joseph had a dream, and he told it to his brothers; and they hated him even more. So he said to them, 'Please hear this dream which I have dreamed: There we were, binding sheaves in the field. Then behold, my sheaf arose and also stood upright; and indeed your sheaves stood all around and bowed down to my sheaf.'*
> *And his brothers said to him, 'Shall you indeed reign over us? Or shall you indeed have dominion over us?' So they hated him even more for his dreams and for his words.*
> *Then he dreamed still another dream and told it to his brothers, and said, 'Look, I have dreamed*

another dream. And this time, the sun, the moon, and the eleven stars bowed down to me.'
So he told it to his father and his brothers; and his father rebuked him and said to him, 'What is this dream that you have dreamed? Shall your mother and I and your brothers indeed come to bow down to the earth before you?' And his brothers envied him, but his father kept the matter in mind.

Genesis 37:2–11

You Have a Purpose

Joseph, like many other Bible characters, was called at a young age; he was only a teenager. The prophet Jeremiah, the prophet Daniel, King David, and even the prophet Samuel were all called at a very young age. This is not to say that God's calling only comes upon the young, as Moses was called at the age of eighty in Exodus 3. Joshua 14:10–11 also says that Caleb, at eighty-five years old, had the same strength as when he was forty years old. God's calling and purpose are for all ages. But the theme of God's calling being on the younger generation tells us that God's plan for people's lives can and most likely is revealed at a very young age.

Look at what God says in Jeremiah 1:4–5, *"Then the word of the Lord came to me, saying: before I formed you in the womb I knew you; before you were born I sanctified you; I ordained you a prophet to the nations."*

Look at what Psalm 139:13, 16 say, *"For You formed my inward parts; you covered me in my mother's womb...Your eyes saw my substance, being yet unformed. And in Your book they all were written, the days fashioned for me, when as yet there were none of them."*

God has a plan and purpose for everyone! If someone is not walking out their God dream, then it is not God's fault; it is theirs. Even Jesus says in Matthew 22:14, *"For many are called, but few are chosen."* The choice is ours whether we want to say yes to God or not. When we look back into our childhood, we can see clear indicators of the plan that God had for our lives once we reached adulthood. Before we do that, let me clarify something. You may be wondering why I began to use the word *calling* when the Genesis text says *dream*. All throughout the Bible, we see that God speaks in various ways, and one of those ways is through dreams. The prophet Daniel, Jacob, Jesus' father Joseph, and obviously Joseph from Genesis, were communicated to by God through dreams. The prophet Ezekiel was shown visions from God, and these are just some of the ways that God communicated to people (Hebrews 1:1).

The dream was a call, a divine invitation that changes the course of one's life for the benefit of others. The dream was simply the form of communication that God used to tell Joseph what his destiny would look like. The interpretation of this dream is revealed later in the Genesis story. For now, I want to focus on the fact that God spoke something to Joseph that gave him purpose and a reason to keep moving forward in life. Even when life becomes extremely difficult, having a vision for your life helps you to keep pressing on!

What's Your Calling?

When I was thirteen years old, I knew my God dream. One morning I was at church. The service began with music as usual, and as usual, I wasn't into it. My twin brother, who was always with my mom and me at church, loved the music part of worship, but he didn't like sitting still and listening to the pastor preach. I was the opposite of him. I struggled to get into the music, but I loved when the Word of God was opened and spoken. On one particular morning, as the pastor preached, I had this burning in my heart to walk up to the platform and talk about God. I literally had to tell myself, "Don't you dare go up there and disrupt the service. Stay in your seat." This began to happen more frequently. This desire to tell people about God began to arise in me more and more. I didn't know what to do with it, and I didn't tell anyone about it. Sadly, I stopped going to church not too long afterward. I began to get distracted with girls, friends, and drugs. When I was nineteen years old, I found myself back in church again.

At age nineteen, I am back in church, hopeful for a better life than the current one I was living. The pastor began to preach, and this prompting surged through my mind, *I am going to do that.* It was that same familiar feeling from when I was thirteen, but that I had forgotten. After the service, I went up to the pastor and thanked him for his message. I then told him, "I think God is calling me to be a pastor." This was the first time I had ever told anyone that. His response back to me was, "Son, it's a lot more difficult than you think." Then he walked away. I was not looking for difficulty, so I didn't give it a second thought. I stopped going to church and once again became distracted by the things of this world. A year and a half later, I was trying to decide which college to transfer to so I could get my bachelor's degree. My mom brought up the idea of going to Bible college. I didn't even know such a place existed. As I looked at their available degrees, they were all geared towards church ministry. So, I said jokingly, "What am I supposed to do, become a pastor?"

A week or so went by, and I was sitting on a couch during my worldly lifestyle, and I received a text message from my mom. She said, "Daniel, I strongly sense that God wants you to be a pastor. You need to pursue this more." As soon as I read that, I texted back, "Don't ever say that to me again. I am not called to be a pastor." I had a high respect for those who did the Lord's work, especially those who taught from God's Word. I did not think that I had the right to even become a pastor because of the poor choices I had made in my life. In my mind, I was a filthy low life. Why would God want anything to do with me? But then, that God's dream began to bubble up and boil over more intensely than ever before, and I could not escape it. His work in my life became more evident in the strangest of ways. Let me explain.

Long Hair Don't Care

I had short hair my entire life, and this new work that God began to do in me made me want to respond in some way. So, I started to grow out my hair. As God began to speak to me about my true identity, I knew that something had to change. What He was doing in my life spiritually began to become evident physically. He was revealing to me that the life I was living was not who I was meant to be (Colossians 3:10). I grew out my hair for six months, and yes, it looked goofy. Some friends of mine were planning on going to a Halloween party, and they invited me. Then they looked at my hair and said, "You should probably get a haircut because no girls are going to talk to you if you look like that." Once I heard that, I went and cut my hair. I went to the party; it was lame, and I just wanted to go home. It was not satisfying, and I began to lose the desire for the old life that I used to live. My hair began to grow out again, and I let it grow, and I did not listen to the opinions of others. I let my hair grow for eight years before I finally cut it for a different reason! I didn't care what others thought about me anymore. I let my hair grow because God was working on a brand-new identity in me, and I wanted to show people in some way that I was serious about what He was doing in my life. I didn't know how else to respond, but I knew I needed to respond in some way. Later in Bible college, my friends called me Samson (for those of you who know that biblical story). The short hair gave me a certain identity that contributed to my old lifestyle. I wanted nothing to do with that old life anymore, and I was quickly losing interest in my old way of living. Even as I grew out my hair, my behavior didn't change immediately. But it was the start of God doing something brand new in me (2 Corinthians 5:17). Are you experiencing something similar? Is God's calling on your life revealing itself to you in the most unexpected of ways?

A Clear Call

As I continued living a worldly lifestyle, the Holy Spirit continued working on my life. As I went to concerts, the Holy Spirit's presence would be with me. As I continued acting on my sinful thoughts, the Holy Spirit would lovingly convict me. As I worked at my retail job, the Holy Spirit spoke through my two Christian co-workers. I then attended the college preview at Multnomah Bible College, still wrestling with God on this pastoral calling, but His Spirit spoke even louder (John 16:8)! I then came to a crossroads, and I had to decide. I cried out to God at around 4 a.m. one morning, and as I earnestly sought Him, I said, "What do I do? Do I go to Multnomah, or do I go to Oregon State?" Oregon State was the other option I was confronted with; if I had made that choice, then I would have continued living my old lifestyle. Then as clear as I have heard anyone speak, I heard an audible voice that said, "You are going to Multnomah, and you are going to be a pastor!" Now I know what you are thinking. How do I know that what I heard was really from God and not my own thoughts? Look at Acts 13:2, *"As they ministered to the Lord and fasted, the Holy Spirit said, 'Now separate to Me Barnabas and Saul for the work to which I have called them.'"* The word Multnomah is nowhere in the Bible. However, Multnomah Bible College was part of the work that God had planned for me, and that University was a part of my training to become a pastor.

I heard this word from the Holy Spirit in February of 2011, and in November of 2014, I was officially ordained a pastor through my church East River Fellowship. So here is my question to you, what is your God dream? Is your current work function giving you that abundant life that Jesus promised? (John 10:10). Do you end your day wishing you could be doing what you really love to do? If you are walking out your God dream, then praise Jesus! But if you are struggling to do so, then I would encourage you to spend time with the Lord. Let Him take you back to your earlier years and allow Him to respeak into your life the God dream He has for you. Go to God and live out His God dream for your life!

Your Calling Will Be Questioned

"Where God puts an exclamation point, the devil puts a question mark."[3]

You also need to know that some people will not immediately believe your God dream. In the case of Joseph and in my own life, that opposition will come from within your own family. Jesus Himself went through this. His own family did not understand His role and mission as the Messiah (John 7:5). After I received my God dream again at twenty years old, I did what Joseph did; I told everyone in my family! I told everyone around me, my community college teachers and classmates, my friends and coworkers, and even strangers. And just like with Joseph, no one believed me or quite understood. I will give you some examples to show you the hardship that you will face when attempting to live out your God dream, especially in the beginning stages. But in these difficult stories, you will also see how powerful God is. I have plenty of encouraging stories as well, where God brought strangers and friends into my path that encouraged me to live for Jesus. God even brought sinners, gangsters, and worldly people into my path, which told me to follow Jesus. Proverbs 16:7 says, *"When a man's ways please the Lord, He makes even his enemies to be at peace with him."*

The opposition to living out my God dream as a pastor came from within my own family and those closest to me at the time. It was the same for Joseph, and it will be the same for you. The enemy will try whatever he can to stop you from starting to walk out your God dream. And he will use those closest to you to do so (Luke 22:3). I want to preface that the stories I am about to share happened at the beginning of my walk with Jesus back in 2011. If my family reads my book today, I don't want to give them the wrong impression that I am ragging on them. My family truly supports me in what I do now. They have provided me with financial, emotional, and spiritual support on many occasions. But it wasn't always like that. I am simply telling the truth of what happened early on in my walk with God. But I can sincerely say that things with my family are different now. They are much better.

It was Halloween night in October 2010. God was stirring up His dream for my life around this time. I was at my sister's house that night, working on a speech for my public speaking class at Portland Community College, due the next morning. A family member of ours came over to visit, and I began to talk with them about me possibly attending Multnomah Bible College. They told me that they knew someone that taught at the school, and they were familiar with the culture at Multnomah. Then they said to me, "The school is not for you. You won't fit in there." This was the beginning of the opposition.

As I began to talk to my other family members, they shared their thoughts and opinions with me, and none of them encouraged me to go to Multnomah Bible College. As I stated earlier, those same family members have been the ones to support me the most out of anyone. But in the beginning, it was tough for my family to understand. Even as I shared my God dream of being a pastor with my friends, they all told me to go to Oregon State instead of Bible College. Even my girlfriend at the time said to me, "You are not called to be a pastor. I know you, and it's not for you."

The last family member that I talked in depth with about the situation was my twin brother. We were driving in my car, and this is what I began to say, "I am going to Multnomah Bible College, I am going to be a pastor, I am going to get off of drugs, I am going to play basketball, and I am going to marry a Christian girl who is a virgin." The reason I said that last part is because God restored to me my purity after I gave my life to Him (1 Corinthians 6:16–17). I was born again (John 3), and I was made brand new (2 Corinthians 5:17)! I didn't think I deserved a wife like that. I was simply expressing the newness of life that God was working in me. This was my brother's response to what I just said, "None of that will ever happen. Once a drug addict, always a drug addict. Why would a girl like that ever marry you? You are going to be with someone just like you were because that's what you deserve." As I was about to drop him off, he was still talking negatively to me. I did the only thing at that moment that I knew to do because my mom used to do this to my siblings and me. I parked the car, looked at my brother, and exclaimed, "In the name of Jesus, Satan flee! For He that is greater in me, is greater than you that is in this world" (Mark 8:31–33; 1 John 4:4). Then I told my brother to get out of my car.

When I got home, I cried. I was so devastated that all this opposition was coming against me, but especially from my own twin brother. Then my phone began to ring, and my twin was calling me. I ignored it until he called me over ten times. I finally answered and asked, "What do you want?" He replied, "Daniel, I don't know what came over me. That didn't seem like me at all." I began to cry, and I said to my brother, "I don't know why no one believes me. I promise on our blood that I am not lying. God spoke to me and told me that I am going to be a pastor. I am just trying to do what He told me to do. But no one believes me." Then my brother said, "Don't let anyone tell you not to follow Jesus. You do what you know you are supposed to do. I'm sorry, Daniel, and I love you."

Stand on the Truth

> *Finally, my brethren, be strong in the Lord and in the power of His might. Put on the whole armor of God, that you may be able to stand against the wiles of the devil. For we do not wrestle against flesh and blood, but against principalities, against powers, against the rulers of the darkness of this age, against spiritual hosts of wickedness in the heavenly places. Therefore take up the whole armor of God, that you may be able to withstand in the evil day, and having done all, to stand. Stand therefore, having girded your waist with truth, having put on the breastplate of righteousness.*

Ephesians 6:10–14

I love my twin brother. This man is the closest person next to me in my life besides Jesus, my wife, and my sons. I had the privilege to officiate his wedding, baptize him and share the Gospel on the street with strangers. He is walking with Jesus today, and my brother loves Jesus and His church! But during the time of the event I just shared, my brother was not walking with Jesus, and the enemy took an opportunity to try to tear me down through him. But I know now that it wasn't my brother speaking to me in that way; it was the enemy. The enemy's tactics didn't work either. I stood on the truth of what God spoke to me, and everything that I told my brother would happen came true! More accurately, everything God told me that would happen came true!

I have been clean and sober since August 2012. I transferred from community college into Multnomah Bible College, and I attended for three years. I played college basketball two out of those three years. I then graduated in May of 2014 from Multnomah University. I was ordained a pastor in November of 2014. I married my beautiful wife, Sonja, on March 5, 2016. She was exactly the woman that I prayed and hoped for. I know I already stated these details in the introduction, but it's worth noting again so we can see the tangibility of God's word coming to pass in my life. Also know, no one can thwart God's plan for your life neither (Job 42:2)! As we will see later in the story of Joseph, we see with Jesus as well; their families believe them and support them in their call. This is the same truth that happened to me, and it will happen for you too.

A true Jesus follower has a vision for their life!

CHAPTER THREE
GIVING IT ALL AWAY

A true Jesus follower gives 100 percent of their life to God!

Let me paraphrase Genesis 37:12–17. Joseph's brothers were feeding their father's flock, and Jacob asked Joseph to go to them. Jacob wanted to make sure that his sons were okay. Shepherding was a dangerous occupation as you were left in an open field all night with wild beasts. So, Joseph went seeking his brothers, and with a little help from a certain man, he found them. Instead of them being in Shechem, they ended up in Dothan. This is what the next part of the text says in Genesis 37,

> *Now when they saw him afar off, even before he came near them, they conspired against him to kill him. Then they said to one another, 'Look, this dreamer is coming! Come therefore, let us now kill him and cast him into some pit; and we shall say, 'Some wild beast has devoured him.' We shall see what will become of his dreams!'*
> *But Reuben heard it, and he delivered him out of their hands, and said, 'Let us not kill him.' And Reuben said to them, 'Shed no blood, but cast him into this pit which is in the wilderness, and do not lay a hand on him'—that he might deliver him out of their hands, and bring him back to his father.*

So it came to pass, when Joseph had come to his brothers, that they stripped Joseph of his tunic, the tunic of many colors that was on him. Then they took him and cast him into a pit. And the pit was empty; there was no water in it. And they sat down to eat a meal.

Genesis 37:18–25a

How would you feel if you were Joseph right now? Probably afraid, lonely, uncertain, and unloved. Joseph was given a God dream, and now he finds himself in a pit all by himself. Unfortunately, this is the beginning of many trials that lay ahead for Joseph until he fulfilled his God dream. Joseph was given a coat of many colors by his father (Genesis 37:3). That coat gave Joseph an identity. It signified that he was loved by his father, that he was set apart from his brothers. We, too, wear things (emotionally, spiritually, and physically) that give us our identity. Just as Joseph's brothers stripped his tunic off from him, we, too, need to be stripped of everything so that we can come to a place where we depend fully on God.

Count the Cost

Right before I heard the Holy Spirit speak to me, "You are going to Multnomah, and you are going to be a pastor" (Acts 13:2), this is what happened. I was working the graveyard shift at Famous Footwear. God was working on my life and nudging me in the right direction to follow Him. However, I was still on the fence as to what I wanted to do. I was stacking shoe boxes, re-organizing the shoe wall, and listening to explicit rap music through my headphones. When suddenly, the Holy Spirit of God began to speak to my conscience, and He said, "Daniel, I need you to break up with your girlfriend as she is not your wife, and she is not part of the plan I have for you. I need you to stop using drugs so when I speak to you, you will know that it is Me that is talking to you. You need to stop smoking cigarettes as well because they are killing you and cutting your life short. They also give you a bad image and make people wonder what else you do besides smoke, and this puts attention on you and not Me. You need to stop listening to your current music selection because it is influencing you and shaping you into someone that you are not supposed to be. You also need to stop cussing, and this will stop when you stop listening to your music." God was asking me to give up my entire life for Him!

Are you willing to give up your entire life to fulfill your God dream?

What was Joseph losing because of pursuing his God dream?

- His brothers
- His father
- His homeland
- His comfort/routine of life

What was Joseph having to face because of pursuing his God dream?

- Isolation
- Fear of the unknown
- Potential death
- Hardship and trials
- Starvation/Poverty
- Abuse

What are you losing/having to face because of pursuing your God dream?

- Career
- Family
- Friends
- Comfort
- Reputation
- Social status

What is it costing you to not fulfill your God dream?

- Greater depth of relationship between you and God
- Pointing others to Jesus
- Joy
- Fulfillment
- An abundant life
- Spirit-led life
- Church family
- Creativity
- Hope

I am not telling you to make a pros-and-cons list to make your decision to follow Jesus with all of your heart. I am asking you to truly consider your current state of living and ask yourself this question, "Am I living out my God dream?" If not, the chances are, there are some things that are holding you back. God has already spoken to you as to what you need to give up and get rid of in your life to pursue Him wholeheartedly.

> *Therefore we also, since we are surrounded by so great a cloud of witnesses, let us lay aside every weight, and the sin which so easily ensnares*

us, and let us run with endurance the race that is set before us, looking unto Jesus, the author and finisher of our faith, who for the joy that was set before Him endured the cross, despising the shame, and has sat down at the right hand of the throne of God.

Hebrews 12:1–2

You need to ask yourself, is what you are holding on to worth not completing what God is asking you to do? One of the major misconceptions with following Jesus is to think that you can still hold on to certain things in your life and get to where He wants to take you. This is not true. You need to give up everything!

God's Grace Is Greater

The first eighteen months of walking with Jesus was amazingly beautiful and yet amazingly difficult. God gave me His supernatural strength to overcome temptations that I once struggled with, drug use, pre-marital sex, depression, anger, selfishness, etc. The problem was that I created habits and a lifestyle that carried over into this new life with Jesus. I wouldn't do drugs for four months, and then I would backslide. I wouldn't smoke cigarettes for six months, and then I would backslide. After a year and a half of walking with Jesus, I found myself backsliding and doing almost everything that God delivered me from eighteen months prior. I remember sitting in my car at the 24-Hour Fitness parking lot. I began to weep as I cried out to God. I was wrestling with two major thoughts that night. First, none of this is real because it's been this long, and I am still living like my old self. Second, I can't do what God has asked me to do. At that very moment, I heard the same voice that I heard from the Holy Spirit at first, but this time He asked me a question. "Do you want to do this or not?" Before I could answer, He said, "If you continue to live this way, I will not work through you."

The Holy Spirit then led me to read Galatians 5:16–26 to confirm what He just spoke. Please take a moment to read it. I remember reading this passage and saying to God, "God, I can't do this. I can't stop living my sinful lifestyle just like that." And the Holy Spirit replied, "You are right. You can't. But I can!" The Lord helped me and cleaned me up again. Then He led me to the church I now attend and where I currently serve as the associate pastor. I remember walking through those church doors in August of 2012. They announced that they were going to have baptisms in October. I had been baptized as a kid but never understood it like I did as an adult. I ended up getting baptized on October 21, 2012, as I committed my life to Jesus wholeheartedly. I still remember standing in that baptismal tub. I was heartbroken that I would backslide on God like that. But I was also serious about following Him, and this was a needed next step. I didn't care about what people thought about me. When I had the chance to share why I was getting baptized that day, I didn't even mention that I was going to school to be a pastor. My focus was on Jesus and truly giving Him 100 percent of my life. I was done messing around. But I needed His help. I knelt in that horse trough filled with water. They dunked me forward, and my head touched the bottom of the tub. My sins were many, so they had to dunk me deeply. But I came out of that water a new man!

A New Creation

My future wife was at East River at the same time I started attending. Her grandmother, who also attends East River, was watching as I stood in the water and shared part of my story with the church. Once I was dunked in the water and came up, my wife's grandmother saw her granddaughter's future husband; it was me. She went and told Sonja (my wife) that God had a man picked out for her. We were married three and a half years later. Did you catch what just happened? As I stood in the water with my junk and sin still attached to me, I was not the proper candidate for my now wife. It was not until I agreed with God to give up everything and to let Him bury my old life. After I came up from the water, the new man arose, and that new man was now fit for God's daughter and Juanita's granddaughter. Romans 6 affirms what I just shared.

The point is this, God has a plan for your life, and it will cost you everything to fulfill it! You need to know that God wants to bless your life (Genesis 1:27–28). He wants to provide for you (Matthew 6:25–34). He also wants you to trust Him and depend on Him. He doesn't want you depending on yourself (Proverbs 3:5–6). It is a continual reliance upon God. He wants that relationship with you. When you give up everything, God gives you everything. What I mean is, He has given us everything we need already (2 Peter 1:3), but to receive it and activate it, we must give all our life to Him! Please take a moment to read these Scriptures in your Bible to encourage you to give God everything: Mark 10:28–30; Philippians 3:12–14; Philippians 2:5–13. Notice the reward for giving Him your all.

A true Jesus follower gives 100 percent of their life to God!

THE
TESTING

CHAPTER FOUR
THE LORD IS WITH YOU

A true Jesus follower has God with them always!

Now Joseph had been taken down to Egypt. And Potiphar, an officer of Pharaoh, captain of the guard, an Egyptian, bought him from the Ishmaelites who had taken him down there. The Lord was with Joseph, and he was a successful man; and he was in the house of his master the Egyptian. And his master saw that the Lord was with him and that the Lord made all he did to prosper in his hand....Then Joseph's master took him and put him into the prison, a place where the king's prisoners were confined. And he was there in the prison. But the Lord was with Joseph and showed him mercy, and He gave him favor in the sight of the keeper of the prison....The keeper of the prison did not look into anything that was under Joseph's authority, because the Lord was with him; and whatever he did, the Lord made it prosper.

Genesis 39:1–3, 20–22, 23

Lost and Found

When I went to the grocery store with my mom as a child, she would tell me not to go in the toy section. We were there for groceries and not toys. This is simply what her budget allowed. But as a child, the temptation grows in you as you desire to at least play with the toys, even if you can't take them home. Normally I wouldn't venture off too far from my mom. But this one time, I did venture away, as the toy section began to call for me like sirens call out to men at sea. My imagination went wild as I played with these toys. As I played, I pondered, *What career path could I pursue as an adult so that I would be able to one day buy all these toys and take them home?* But then I realized something, *Where is my mom?* Panic and fear began to creep into my heart as I realized I had lost her. I thought, *Surely she will come looking for me.* But as time went by, she never came to the toy section. She did tell me not to go there, so my mom obviously trusted that I would listen to her. Now, this makes it even worse as I did what she told me not to do. As I sat there lost, scared, and away from my mom, I suddenly heard my name over the telecom speaker, "Daniel, please come to check stand 5; your mother is here. Daniel, please come to check stand 5." Now, if I was a teenager, then this would have been embarrassing. Since I was still a little boy, joy welled up in me as I ran to the check stand. Yes, I got disciplined when we got home. But it felt good to not be lost and to be with mom again.

Sometimes we feel like that lost kid in the grocery store when it comes to our relationship with God. As soon as we get into dire predicaments, we think God is not with us and that He distances from us. But Joseph didn't think like that. Genesis 37:25–36 reveals the struggle that his brothers had when it came to disposing of Joseph. Joseph was not killed by his brothers; rather, he was sold into slavery. God spared Joseph, and instead of letting him die, he continued to live, but it was in a foreign land with much trouble ahead. Joseph was sold as a slave in a foreign land as a teenager. He was wrongly convicted by his new master's wife and thrown into prison as a result. If you were sold into a foreign land and thrown into prison on false accusations, would you begin to doubt God is with you? Before I knew that trials were part of my Jesus journey, I would have doubted that God was truly with me. I thought trials meant He left me. But just like my mom in the grocery store, God is always there. He too calls out to His children to come back to Him (Zechariah 1:3)! Genesis 39:1–3, 20–22, 23 clearly states that God was with Joseph. How was God with him? His master Potiphar even saw with his own eyes that God was with Joseph. There was tangible evidence that God was involved in Joseph's life.

God's Presence at a Party

I gave my life to Jesus just three months away from being twenty-one years old. My twin brother's co-workers planned a party for his twenty-first birthday, and I was invited along. I didn't want to go as I was newly saved, but I went to support my brother on our birthday. Immediately the party began, and everyone began to drink alcohol. People offered me liquor, beer, my favorite brand of cigarettes, marijuana, hard core drugs, sex, etc. I turned it all down. People were amazed at my response because they knew the old me. I heard one person say to another, "Man, Daniel is really serious about not doing any of this. He has a strong will." I stood with my back against one of the walls and began to cry. No one noticed because they were all drunk and under the influence of other drugs. But I cried because I knew it wasn't by my will or strength that I resisted. It was because of who was in me (Zechariah 4:6).

I cried and said to the Lord, "Lord God, if they would have offered me this three months ago, I would have said yes. The only reason I turned it all down is because you have given me the strength to say no and overcome these temptations. I'm so sorry, Lord, that people think it's me saying no, and they can't see that it's You who is helping me." That's why I cried. Because people didn't realize that it was the strength of God in me, and He empowered me to refuse the things I enjoyed in my old life before Christ (Romans 6). The reason I bring this story up is to affirm that there is evidence of God's presence in our lives. How have you experienced God's presence in your life? We know God is with us and others do as well!

How Can We Know for Certain That the Lord Is Always with Us?

Jesus said in Matthew 28:20b, *"And lo (surely), I am with you always, even to the end of the age. Amen."* Acts 1 says that Jesus is now at the right hand of the Father in heaven. So how can Jesus be with us always? In John 14:16–18, Jesus tells His disciples that He is about to go to the Father who sent Him. He told them not to be troubled for this reason:

> *And I will pray the Father, and He will give you another Helper, that He may abide with you forever— the Spirit of truth, whom the world*

cannot receive, because it neither sees Him nor knows Him; but you know Him, for He dwells with you and will be in you. I will not leave you orphans; I will come to you.

John 14:16–18

Notice how Jesus says, "You know Him (the Holy Spirit), for He dwells with you." Jesus chose to rely on the power of the Holy Spirit to fulfill His ministry (Matthew 12:28). Therefore, the disciples have seen the Holy Spirit move in their midst. So they are familiar with Him.

But Jesus takes it one step further and says, "And will be in you." How much closer can God be to us than in us? In John 1:14, it says that *"The Word (Jesus) became flesh and dwelt among us."* Becoming His own creation in the form of a human is close (Philippians 2). But now God resides in us; hence He is with us always! *"Do you not know that you are the temple of God and that the Spirit of God dwells in you?"* (1 Corinthians 3:16). *"Or do you not know that your body is the temple of the Holy Spirit who is in you, whom you have from God, and you are not your own?"* (1 Corinthians 6:19). When you have the Holy Spirit in you, you can be certain that the LORD is always with you!

How Do We Let God In?

Then Peter said to them, "Repent, and let every one of you be baptized in the name of Jesus Christ for the remission of sins; and you shall receive the gift of the Holy Spirit. For the promise is to you and to your children, and to all who are afar off, as many as the Lord our God will call.

Acts 2:38–39

1. *We must repent.*[4] Repent means to make a change in mind and action. To turn from the road you are currently traveling and to turn to God and follow Him (Matthew 7:13–14)!

This makes me think of marriage. When I stood at the altar with my soon-to-be wife, I had to decide what I wanted. That decision meant that I was forsaking all past relationships and all future relationships and was committing to her only. If I was not willing to do so, then my wife wouldn't be able to give all herself to me. She was committing to be with me and only me. If I wasn't willing to reciprocate the same commitment, then we would ultimately disagree, and the relationship would fall apart soon afterward. So, the question we have to answer is, do we want God? Do we truly believe that God is enough for us? When you think about the Holy Spirit entering your life and wanting to stay forever, does it excite you or scare you? Do you want God with you always? Some people may not want this commitment because that means that their lifestyle has to change.

The Choice Is Yours

In my bachelor-like living, I was empty, unsatisfied, and lonely. The life I was living as a single man was not what I wanted for the rest of my life. I had a choice to make. Do I keep living like this, or do I make a change? I asked the Lord what I should do, and as clear as day, I heard in my spirit, "Get married!" This commitment changed the trajectory of my life. I was no longer steeped in sexual sin (more on this topic later). I was able to find comfort, trust, and security in every aspect of my life by being with my wife and her only. But I had to desire this change. I honestly didn't realize how difficult marriage would be, but I can tell you truthfully with all my heart, it is well worth the sacrifice! When the Holy Spirit comes into your life, things will change. His desires start to become your desires. His ways become your ways. If we are not willing to partner with Him and let Him lead our lives, then He is not going to force Himself on us. So, the question is, do you want God? Would if the love of your life walked down the wedding aisle and asked you in front of everyone, "Do you want to be with me?" And your response back was, "I'm not sure." Or "I'm not fully willing." Then chances are, you wouldn't get married that day. If you truly want God in your life, then you have to not only be willing to repent, but you have to repent. Especially if this relationship with God is going to work in the long run.

2. *We must be baptized.*[5] To be baptized simply means to dip, immerse, to be cleansed or purified by washing.

I want to note here that baptism is a truth displayed throughout the entire Bible, both Old and New Testaments. When Israel crossed over the Red Sea in Exodus 14, Paul references this event as an act of baptism in 1 Corinthians 10:1–4. The children of Israel were leaving their old lives of slavery behind. They went through the water of the Red Sea. Their enemies and anything that represented their old lives were covered by the water and didn't continue with them. Then they moved forward into the desert and began a new journey headed to the promised land. That is what a new life in Jesus is all about! Out with the old and in with the new! All that is represented in water baptism. I wanted to point this out before I continue with this next part because you may wonder as you read, how did we go from talking about the Lord being with Joseph in the Book of Genesis to baptism in the Book of Acts?

Joseph had the Holy Spirit in him (Genesis 41:38). This meant that God was always with him. You want God with you always, too, right? Then you need the Holy Spirit in you! Baptism is part of receiving the Holy Spirit into your life. When you have the Holy Spirit in you, you can be assured that God is always with you! Baptism is a truth throughout the entire Bible. Even Peter in 1 Peter 3:20–21 references the story of Noah in Genesis 6–8, as it being a baptism. The Lord showed me something from Noah's Ark story that I would like to share with you.

Is the Holy Spirit Clear for Landing on Your Life?

I was reading the story of Noah and the flood in Genesis 8, and the Holy Spirit opened my eyes to the importance of receiving Him into our lives. Please take a moment to read in your Bible Genesis 8:6–12. This reminded me of Jesus' baptism too:

> *When He had been baptized, Jesus came up immediately from the water; and behold, the heavens were opened to Him, and He saw the Spirit of God descending like a dove and alighting upon Him. And suddenly a voice came from heaven, saying, 'This is My beloved Son, in whom I am well pleased.'*

> **Matthew 3:16–17**

Notice that the dove could only rest on the land when the waters had receded. Notice that the Holy Spirit only rested upon Jesus once He came up from the water. What

God revealed to me through these passages of Scripture is that many Jesus followers are lacking His presence in their lives because they are still under the water (metaphorically speaking). The Holy Spirit can only dwell on what has come up and out of the water. Sure, there are exceptions like Samson in the Book of Judges. But the story of Samson is about God's faithfulness during our faithlessness. The Holy Spirit moving in the life of Samson had nothing to do with his righteousness. It had everything to do with the righteous character of God to keep His promises to His people. The Holy Spirit can't rest on you if you are still under the water, living in your old life. The Holy Spirit will only rest on you when you leave your old self in the water and trust God to help you live new! Live a life worthy of repentance. Come up and out of the water!

Being baptized is more than being dunked in water as a religious act. When we commit to baptism, we are committing to Jesus! We are making a public declaration of our faith in Jesus. We are not getting dunked in water to just have a better life. We are stating that our sinful, wicked, dark, evil, old self is dying. As the water represents the grave/the ground, our old self is going under. As we come up from the water, our new self is emerging (Romans 6)! Water alone can't save you. Water alone can't wash away all our sins and get us right with God.

Why Water?

Water is the physical representation of what is taking place inside us. Outwardly the water represents cleansing, purifying, washing away, etc. But what the water is doing on the outside, the Holy Spirit has done on the inside (Titus

3:5). John 3 also tells us that we must be born again to enter the kingdom of God. And the only way we are getting into heaven is if we have that seal of the Holy Spirit on our lives (Ephesians 1:13–14). Think about this for a moment. When we came into this world, we came in blood and water from our mother's womb. I know, I just went there. But bear with me. I watched as both of my sons came into this world through blood and water. Even though children are innocent (Romans 9:11), they are still born into sin (Psalm 51:5). Therefore, Jesus says in John 3 that we must be born again. And just like Nicodemus, I ask the same question, *"How can a man be born when he is old? Can he enter a second time into his mother's womb and be born?"* (John 3:4). Then Jesus gives us the answer, *"Most assuredly, I say to you, unless one is born of water and the Spirit, he cannot enter the kingdom of God"* (John 3:5). Right before my wife delivered our second son Elisha, they broke her water. They told her that very soon after that, the baby would come. That meant that this new little life was about to emerge into this world. It's the same thing with water baptism. Once we break through the water, a new life springs forth!

Notice that Jesus says one must be born of water and the Spirit. The Spirit is the agent that is doing the cleaning and purifying work in our heart, soul, and spirit.

> *But when the kindness and the love of God our Savior toward man appeared, not by works of righteousness which we have done, but according to His mercy He saved us, through the washing of regeneration and renewing of the Holy Spirit, whom He poured out on us abundantly through Jesus Christ our Savior, that having been justified*

by His grace we should become heirs according
to the hope of eternal life.

Titus 3:4–7

Regeneration means new birth.[6] Renewal means brand new.[7] This is done by the Holy Spirit and not the water alone. No, we can't go back into our mother's womb and come forth in the water again. But as the church sets water before people, it provides an opportunity for them to be born again, of water and the Spirit.

At this point, you may be wondering, do I have to be water baptized to receive the Holy Spirit? Do I have to be water baptized to be saved and go to heaven? The short answer to both those questions is no. Water can't save you. It takes the blood of Jesus (Hebrews 9:22) and the washing of the Holy Spirit to clean us up, as we just discussed above. Two examples come to mind: the thief on the cross next to Jesus and the Gentiles in Acts 10.

God Just Wants Your Heart

Then one of the criminals who were hanged blasphemed Him, saying, 'If You are the Christ, save Yourself and us.' But the other, answering, rebuked him, saying, 'Do you not even fear God, seeing you are under the same condemnation? And we indeed justly, for we receive the due reward of our deeds; but this Man has done nothing wrong.' Then he said to Jesus, 'Lord, remember me when You come into Your kingdom.' And Jesus said to him, 'Assuredly, I say to you, today you will be with Me in Paradise.'

Luke 23:39–43

67

This is a clear act of repentance by one of the thieves on the cross. He admitted his faults, He believed in Jesus, and He asked for forgiveness, and Jesus responded back by saying, "You will be with Me in paradise (heaven)." Jesus did not say, "Get off the cross and be baptized first, and then you can enter heaven with Me." Not saying this to be funny, but that would have been difficult for the man to have done so, considering he is about to die on the cross. God looks upon the heart (1 Samuel 16:7).

Romans 10:9–10 says that *"If you confess with your mouth the Lord Jesus and believe in your heart that God has raised Him from the dead, you will be saved. For with the heart one believes unto righteousness, and with the mouth confession is made unto salvation."* The thief did just that, and on the cross, he was immediately sealed with the Holy Spirit (Ephesians 1:13–14), which granted him access into eternity with God the Father through Jesus (Ephesians 2:18). He was not water baptized and still went to heaven.

No Water No Problem

The other example that comes to mind is in Acts 10. Peter receives a vision to go and speak to the Gentiles about Jesus.

> *While Peter was still speaking these words, the Holy Spirit fell upon all those who heard the word. And those of the circumcision who believed were astonished, as many as came with Peter, because the gift of the Holy Spirit had been poured out on the Gentiles also. For they heard them speak with tongues and magnify God. Then Peter answered, 'Can anyone forbid water, that these should not be baptized who have received the Holy Spirit*

*just as we have?' And he commanded them to be
baptized in the name of the Lord. Then they asked
him to stay a few days.*

Acts 10:44–48

The Gentiles received the Holy Spirit before they were water baptized! Peter was preaching the gospel to them, and the Holy Spirit came on them. Galatians 3:5 says, *"Therefore He who supplies the Spirit to you and works miracles among you, does He do it by the works of the law, or by the hearing of faith?"* The Gentiles belonged to God the moment the Holy Spirit came on them. Peter said in Acts 2:38 that salvation comes from repentance and the gift of the Holy Spirit. Amen! But Peter doesn't let them off the hook. He still commands them to be water baptized! A friend of mine had an encounter like this, where he was filled with the Spirit before water baptism, and he asked me this question, "Daniel, since I am now saved, why do I need to get water baptized?" That's a good question. And my response was, "It's about obedience."

Obedience

In the story of Elisha and the leper in 2 Kings 5, Naaman the leper was told by Elisha to go dip seven times in the Jordan River to be healed. Naaman became upset that this was required for his healing. He wanted Elisha to simply say a few words, wave his hand over him and heal him. But it comes down to obedience. Are we willing to do what God tells us to do? Naaman's servant talks him into it, and once Naaman obeys, his healing comes! This is a clear picture for us today that we, too, need to obey God when He asks something of us. Water is obviously meaningful to God. Water is part of our earthly birth, and it is part of our spiritual birth. God does not want us to do a religious act to simply please Him. He wants us to trust Him and believe Him in what He says. I heard someone say it like this, "If you are not willing to get your hair wet for God, then what else are you not willing to do for Him?" It comes down to obedience.

The blood of Jesus and the Holy Spirit cleans us up! Water solidifies the spiritual work that God has done on the inside. While water baptism is not necessarily required for salvation, nor required to be filled with the Spirit, it is commanded by God for us to do. Therefore, it deems great importance for us to obey Him in this command. If water is available, then we need to be baptized. This is one way we can be certain that we receive the Holy Spirit, who then dwells with us forever. The Spirit's presence in your life affirms that the LORD is with you always! God was with Joseph in tangible ways, and once you accept Him into your heart, then God is with you in tangible ways as well. The most tangible way is that He put His Holy Spirit in you!

Spirit-Filled

My personal experience of being filled with the Holy Spirit happened when I was water baptized. I experienced exactly what Acts 2:38–39 describes. I repented, got baptized, and received the Holy Spirit! After I was baptized, I couldn't stop singing. As I lay in my bed that night, I continued singing. I couldn't sleep! I had school the next day, and I kept on singing. Twenty-four hours later, I finally stopped singing and humming and praising God. I was so joyful! I told everyone I talked to about my recent experience. I wasn't sure what to make of it, but then the Holy Spirit led me to read this scripture,

> *And do not be drunk with wine, in which is dissipation; but be filled with the Spirit, speaking to one another in psalms and hymns and spiritual songs, singing and making melody in your heart to the Lord, giving thanks always for all things to God the Father in the name of our Lord Jesus Christ, submitting to one another in the fear of God.*

Ephesians 5:18–21

This was proof that I had been filled with the Holy Spirit! From that day forward, I was completely changed. I never touched a drug from that point on, and I have never had the power on my own to do that before. Being an ex-drug addict may not be your story. But in what ways have you seen God move in power in your life? Having the Holy Spirit in you gives you full assurance of the LORD being with you always. How was Joseph able to turn from sexual sin and not commit adultery with his master's wife? How was Joseph able to serve his master faithfully without grumbling or complaining? How was Joseph able to serve the warden in prison? How was Joseph able to accomplish such great things? Genesis 41:38 says, *"And Pharaoh said to his servants, 'Can we find such a one as this, a man in whom is the Spirit of God?'"* Joseph had the Holy Spirit in him. The presence of God enabled Joseph to achieve those tasks. God was with him wherever he went!

A true Jesus follower has God with them always!

CHAPTER FIVE
SEXUAL SIN

A true Jesus follower flees sexual sin!

> *Now Joseph was handsome in form and appearance. And it came to pass after these things that his master's wife cast longing eyes on Joseph, and she said, 'Lie with me.' But he refused and said to his master's wife, 'Look, my master does not know what is with me in the house, and he has committed all that he has to my hand. There is no one greater in this house than I, nor has he kept back anything from me but you, because you are his wife. How then can I do this great wickedness, and sin against God?' So it was, as she spoke to Joseph day by day, that he did not heed her, to lie with her or to be with he...But it happened about this time, when Joseph went into the house to do his work, and none of the men of the house was inside, that she caught him by his garment, saying, 'Lie with me.' But he left his garment in her hand, and fled and ran outside.*

Genesis 39:6b–12

Be Careful What You See

I remember the first time I was introduced to pornography.

I was ten years old, and one of our neighborhood friends found his brother's porn DVD. As I watched what was on the screen, I had no idea what was happening. I could not comprehend the idea of sex at that young of an age. As I hit puberty around twelve years old, my desires began to change. That is when I masturbated for the first time. I wasn't watching anything pornographic while this happened. It simply happened out of curiosity. This pleasure opened a door for me, and I had no idea where it was going to lead. All I knew was that it felt good. And at that young of an age, I didn't feel any guilt about it. This led to watching more pornography, and eventually, it led to sexual acts with girls in our neighborhood. At fourteen years old, I gave over my virginity and had sex for the first time. My mom told my brother and me not to engage in sexual activity before we were married. She warned us we could get sexually transmitted diseases, we could get a girl pregnant, and she explained to us the emotional and spiritual consequences behind sexual activity outside of marriage (1 Corinthians 6:15–20). The problem was, I didn't experience any of those things, even after having sex with multiple people. I believed my mom, but I just thought I was the exception to the rule. I continued this sexual lifestyle until I was almost twenty-one years old.

A Sticky Situation

Just because I didn't experience any immediate consequences, that doesn't mean that I didn't experience problems later. There were consequences for my behavior. *"Or do you not know that he who is joined to a harlot is one body with her? For "the two," He says, "shall become one flesh." But he who is joined to the Lord is one spirit with*

Him" (1 Corinthians 6:16–17). To put this verse into an easy understanding for us, it's like taking a piece of tape, sticking it to something, and ripping it off, over and over and over. Sooner or later, the tape loses its stickiness and becomes useless for its original purpose. That's what happens to us when we give ourselves to people before marriage. We take pieces of them and transfer them to ourselves and then to others. That's scary to think about. This is where connections are formed and emotions are bonded together. I suffered severe emotional consequences for the decisions I made. Like someone once told me, "I made a connection where I shouldn't have."

The truth is, even if you stop being with those people on your own, they are still stuck to you in some way. We need to repent and turn to Jesus. He will take that old, battered down, and used piece of us and make us brand new (2 Corinthians 5:17)! He makes us useful again! That's amazing news for you and your future spouse. I won't go into too much detail because it hurts my heart to even talk about it. But even after I married my amazing wife, I still had to deal with those emotional consequences from my past. But now, another innocent person (my wife) was involved in my healing process. She was now in the crossfires of my past decisions. The things I did at twelve years old affected me as a twenty-five-year-old newly married man. Here are some examples of lingering consequences that I have had to work through in my marriage:

- going on a casual walk with my wife and seeing people from my past walk right by us;
- my wife bringing up baby names for our children and those names triggering moments from my past; and

- avoiding going into a store with my wife because I saw someone from my past.

As my wife tells me all the time, "You are covered by Jesus," it still hurts me to have my wife go through that stuff. If I could go back, I wouldn't have made the decisions I made when I was younger. You know the consequences are real when what you chose to do as a teenager impacts you as an adult. It's better to do things God's way from the very beginning. There is always hope to have Jesus turn this situation of your life around; He did for mine. Yet, there are always consequences for what we do. We reap what we sow (Galatians 6:8).

Life's Not Fair

My mindset towards sex outside of marriage began to change because of two encounters that I had: one physical and one spiritual. At eighteen years old, one of my glands got infected because of a cut I obtained inside of my mouth. The gland in my neck swelled up like a mini balloon. It scared me, so I went to the doctor. Their first question to me was, "Are you sexually active?" I replied, "Yes." Then they asked me if I had ever been tested for sexually transmitted diseases. I said "No," and they seemed concerned and sure that I had acquired one. I was nervous as I sat in that office. They ran the tests and told me that they would contact me soon. I thought, *What have I done? Everything my mom said is about to come true.* I got the call later that day, and the report came back negative. The swelling in my gland had to do with an infection that did not come from sexual activity. They prescribed me antibiotics, and it was resolved shortly after. I was relieved, to say the least. But then I was puzzled.

How could I have slept with all those girls and not have received a sexually transmitted disease? It didn't seem fair. I deserved to have something bad happen to me because of my decisions. Though what my mom taught me didn't happen, that's what caught my attention. I didn't deserve to have been protected like that when I was clearly making wrong decisions. It's sad to say, but this moment did not stop me from being sexually active. But it did help me for the next encounter I had, which was the spiritual encounter.

Breaking God's Heart

I was twenty years old and still doing the same old thing. But because of a broken heart and broken dreams at the age of nineteen years old, the Holy Spirit began to minister to my heart again. I was more open because the plans for my life had failed. While I was amid this sinful lifestyle, I heard in my spirit, "What you are doing is wrong, and it's wrong against Me!" Hold up! What was that? I was still using drugs at this time in my life, and for the first time at twenty years old, I thought I had taken too many. All I knew was that what I heard did not come from me. I found out later that a similar situation happened to a man named Saul (the Apostle Paul) in the Bible.

> As he journeyed he came near Damascus, and suddenly a light shone around him from heaven. Then he fell to the ground, and heard a voice saying to him, 'Saul, Saul, why are you persecuting Me?' And he said, 'Who are You, Lord?' the Lord said, 'I am Jesus, whom you are persecuting. It is hard for you to kick against the goads.' So he, trembling and astonished, said, 'Lord, what do You want me to do?' Then the Lord said to him,

'Arise and go into the city, and you will be told what you must do.'

Acts 9:3–6

For the first time in my life, I realized that I had broken God's heart (Genesis 6:5–6). My first thought was, Jesus, you have never done anything to hurt me, so I don't want to do anything to hurt you. God made a boundary, and I trespassed on it. I didn't go against religion; I went against a relationship. There is Someone on the other end of this thing we call Christianity. That Someone created you and I. King David came to the same conclusion in Psalm 51:3–4 when he said, *"For I acknowledge my transgressions, And my sin is always before me. Against You, You only, have I sinned, And done this evil in Your sight—That You may be found just when You speak, And blameless when You judge."* King David committed adultery and many other extreme sins in 2 Samuel 11, and God confronted him through one of His prophets in 2 Samuel 12, and this is where we get the cry of David's heart from Psalm 51.

Sex Is Good

Sex is not bad! I want to make that clear. It is a pet peeve of mine when Christ followers tell people, "Sex is bad." Sex is a good thing. God created sex (Genesis 2:25). God condones sex (Genesis 1:28). Sex is not good when it takes place outside of marriage, a covenant relationship between a man and a woman. Any sexual act outside of marriage between a man and a woman is a sin. This is known as sexual immorality (1 Corinthians 6:18; Hebrews 13:4; 1 Thessalonians 4:3–5). Notice that Joseph was not fleeing the act of sex from his wife (he was not married at this time), but he was fleeing the act of sex with another man's wife. In this case, it was his master Potiphar's wife. He was fleeing sexual sin. Joseph responds to her with this, "How then can I do this great wickedness and sin against God?" Why is having sex with someone else's spouse considered great wickedness and sin? Hebrews 13:4 says, *"Let marriage be held in honor among all, and let the marriage bed be undefiled, for God will judge the sexually immoral and adulterous."* The reason adultery (having sex with another person's spouse) is wrong is because God Himself has commanded it so. God desires oneness between a husband and a wife because He Himself is One (Deuteronomy 6:4). God has set a standard for mankind to follow in sex and in all areas of life. He has done so for our good (Deuteronomy 10:12–13).

Did God Really Say?

Even after having these two encounters with the LORD, I still questioned His standard. Is having sex outside of marriage wrong? So, I asked the LORD, "Where does it say sex outside of marriage is wrong in your Word?" Be careful what you ask for because He will answer you! Please take a moment to read in your Bible 1 Thessalonians 4:1–8. There you have it, folks. I could share so many more scriptures to affirm the truth that sexual immorality is a sin. But this passage from 1 Thessalonians 4 hit me right in the heart. It was so clear, and now it demanded a response from me. Was I going to continue living against God's standard? Or would I submit to His ways? The Holy Spirit also led me to Galatians 5:16-26, as I mentioned in a previous chapter, *"Those who practice such things will not inherit the kingdom of God."* God loved me enough to tell me the truth. If I kept living the way I was living, then I wouldn't be able to live with Him in heaven for the rest of eternity. For James 5:17 says, *"Therefore, to him who knows to do good and does not do it, to him it is sin."* Sin separates us from God and does not allow us to be in His presence (Isaiah 59:2).[8] Sin simply means missing the mark. The Bible makes it clear that we all have missed the mark (Romans 3:23).

What Now?

At the end of that 1 Thessalonians 4 passage, verse 7 says, "…who has given us His Holy Spirit." The Holy Spirit not only gives us the power to overcome sin (Zechariah 4:6), but He leads us into new life (Psalm 143:10) and speaks truth to us along the way (John 16:13). We are not alone in overcoming sexual sin. For God is with us! God isn't going to ask us to do something without equipping us to do it. God never told me to stop having sex. God asked me if I would do things His way. As I was convicted of my sexual sin, the Lord told me that I would continue having sex because He has put that desire in me (Genesis 1:28). However, my sexual desire was misplaced and hence was not right before God. The only way my sex life would be blessed by God is if I got married. Sex is acceptable in marriage alone. Marriage between a man and woman, as I explained earlier. Sex in marriage is meant for connection between husband and wife, is meant for producing children, and is meant for protection; physically, emotionally, and spiritually. The answer for me was not to quit having sex. The answer was to get married (1 Corinthians 7)! I took God up on His Word, and I am now living a blessed life with the love of my life!

Having the Talk

This topic of sexuality is most important to me because it's one area where I see Jesus' followers corrupt the most. These are people who proclaim to follow Jesus but don't follow His commands (John 14:15). I was out in the streets sharing Jesus when I ran into a young guy who I saw wearing a cross necklace. As soon as I started talking to him about Jesus, he rolled up his shirt sleeve and showed me a cross tattooed on his arm as well. But as we continued our conversation, he revealed to me that he had a girlfriend and was currently having sex with her. I told him that I used to wear a cross necklace and I have a cross tattoo on my back, and yet I used to do the same thing as him. I told him that the cross represents us dying to our old self and living new for Jesus (Galatians 2:20). So, who is still living in you, the old self or the new self? He was convicted of his sin, just like I was all those years ago. I told him how important it is for us who proclaim to follow Jesus, to be a Christ-like example to others.

We can't tell people we follow Jesus and then not do what He says. Luke 6:46 says, *"Why do you call Me Lord, Lord and not do the things which I say?"* I told him that God desires that he breaks up with his girlfriend or he marries her. He said he knew that his girlfriend was not his wife. So, I prayed that he would have the courage to cut off the relationship. Because the reality is, if that girl isn't his wife, then she is some other man's wife. I had to do the same thing with my past relationship before my wife. God told me that my ex-girlfriend wasn't my wife and wasn't part of my future. More than two years later, I met Sonja, and a little over two years after that, we got married. It took nearly five years for me to finally have a wife after I obeyed God. But it was well worth the wait because I am no longer breaking God's heart, and I am now blessed by God in marriage (Proverbs 18:22)!

A Sympathetic Savior

Where are you at when it comes to sexual sin? Are you looking at pornography? Are you masturbating? Are you committing adultery? Are you having sex outside of marriage? Are you struggling with same-sex attraction? Wherever you are on the scale, God wants to help you and bless you. He knows that the struggle is real.

> *Seeing then that we have a great High Priest who has passed through the heavens, Jesus the Son of God, let us hold fast our confession. For we do not have a High Priest who cannot sympathize with our weaknesses, but was in all points tempted as we are, yet without sin. Let us therefore come boldly to the throne of grace, that we may obtain mercy and find grace to help in time of need.*

Hebrews 4:14–16

Jesus went through temptation and yet didn't sin. He relied on the same Holy Spirit that we rely on today to overcome temptation. Jesus knows how weak the flesh is, so He knows how to help you. Do you want God's help? Do you want to flee from sexual sin? Then run to the God who created you and ask Him for His help. When we sin, we sin against God, just like Joseph said. My prayer is that you would have this heart, "Jesus, you have never done anything to hurt me, so I don't want to do anything to hurt You."

A true Jesus follower flees sexual sin!

CHAPTER SIX
YOU ARE GIFTED

A true Jesus follower functions in spiritual gifts!

To summarize the end of Genesis 39 and the beginning of Genesis 40, Joseph ends up in prison. Potiphar's wife did not get Joseph like she wanted, and she falsely accused him of trying to rape her. Joseph should have died, but he was put in prison and was then put in charge of the prison. God blessed him no matter what circumstance he found himself in. The king's butler and the king's baker end up in prison for upsetting the Pharaoh. God works through Joseph, which gets Pharaoh's attention and eventually leads to Joseph being freed from prison. But before Joseph was released from prison, God had an assignment for Joseph to fulfill.

Then the butler and the baker of the king of Egypt, who were confined in the prison, had a dream, both of them, each man's dream in one night and each man's dream with its own interpretation. And Joseph came in to them in the morning and looked at them, and saw that they were sad. So he asked Pharaoh's officers who were with him in the custody of his lord's house, saying, 'Why do you look so sad today?' And they said to him, 'We each have had a dream, and there is no interpreter of it.' So Joseph said to them, 'Do not interpretations belong to God? Tell them to me, please.'

Genesis 40:5–8

Dreams

If interpretations of dreams belong to God, then why would Joseph tell these two men to tell him their dreams? First off, Joseph had experienced dreams and interpretations before. He received two dreams from God when he was seventeen years old. Second, he trusted that God would entrust him with these dream interpretations, just like He did with his own dreams. Joseph was gifted by God to interpret dreams! So the chief butler tells Joseph his dream, and Joseph replies, "This is the interpretation of it" (verse 12). Then the baker tells Joseph his dream, and Joseph replies, "This is the interpretation of it" (verse 18). Both of their dreams came true! One worked out for the one, and for the other, not so much. You can read Genesis 40 to see what happened to the baker and the butler. But God didn't stop there with Joseph's gift. Pharaoh ends up having two dreams, and he can't find anyone in his kingdom to interpret them (Genesis 41:8). But God worked through Joseph to give Pharaoh his dream interpretation!

Then it came to pass, at the end of two full years, that Pharaoh had a dream; and behold, he stood by the river...Then Pharaoh sent and called Joseph, and they brought him quickly out of the dungeon; and he shaved, changed his clothing, and came to Pharaoh. And Pharaoh said to Joseph, 'I have had a dream, and there is no one

> *who can interpret it. But I have heard it said of*
> *you that you can understand a dream, to interpret*
> *it.' So Joseph answered Pharaoh, saying, 'It is*
> *not in me; God will give Pharaoh an answer of*
> *peace.'*

Genesis 41:1, 14–16

Before the butler and the baker leave the prison, Joseph tells the butler to put a good word in for him so that he too can get out of prison. The butler doesn't, and Joseph was forgotten in prison for another two years! But when Pharaoh couldn't find anyone in his kingdom to interpret his dreams, then the butler remembers Joseph. He tells Pharaoh about him, and this is why Pharaoh calls for Joseph. Joseph gets out of prison, and he interprets Pharaoh's two dreams. This is how Pharaoh responds in Genesis 41:38–39, "And Pharaoh said to his servants, *'Can we find such a one as this, a man in whom is the Spirit of God?'* Then Pharaoh said to Joseph, *"In as much as God has shown you all this, there is no one as discerning and wise as you.'"*

Gifts from Above

Romans 11:29 says, *"For the gifts and the calling of God are irrevocable."* This means that when God gives you a spiritual gift, it is unchangeable; it stays with you. I have heard of missionaries speaking in a foreign language to minister to the people of that land, even though the missionaries never learned the language. This was supernatural, and Acts 2 affirms this experience. However, those missionaries never had that happen to them again, nor did they come to be fluent in that language after their experience. This is a miracle from God! But when you notice a consistent pattern of a spiritual act in your life, it is most likely a spiritual gift from God. A spiritual gift can't be earned, but it can be sought after (1 Corinthians 14:1,12). It is first given by God alone (1 Corinthians 12:11), and then you can grow in that gift the more you exercise it, like working out a muscle (Romans 12:6–8). The reason why the Bible calls them spiritual gifts is because it's a gift beyond your own ability. The prophet Daniel in Daniel 2 was also gifted in dream interpretation. King Nebuchadnezzar had a dream, but he wanted his magicians and wise men to tell him the dream first and then give him the interpretation. His people couldn't do it, but God worked through the prophet Daniel, and not only did he give Nebuchadnezzar the interpretation, but he first told him verbatim what his dream was! What a gift from God! First Corinthians 12:7 says that each one of us has a spiritual gift from God! Once we discover what our gifts are, then we are told to walk in them (1 Peter 4:10–11).

There are plenty of "spiritual gift" tests that you can take to discover your spiritual gifts. I am not against those. But I would encourage you to seek in the scriptures what spiritual gifts are available to us and then check to see if you have seen any of them in your life. If you haven't seen a certain spiritual gift in your life, it does not mean that you don't have that gift. You could discover it later in life. If you have a desire for it, then ask God for it (1 Corinthians 12:31). Ask until He tells you no. But remember, spiritual gifts are not for you; they are for others (1 Corinthians 14:12). Spiritual gifts are not meant to make us feel more valuable; they are meant to give God glory! Functioning in spiritual gifts points people to God.

But if all prophesy, and an unbeliever or an uninformed person comes in, he is convinced by all, he is convicted by all. And thus the secrets of his heart are revealed; and so, falling down on his face, he will worship God and report that God is truly among you. How is it then, brethren? Whenever you come together, each of you has a psalm, has a teaching, has a tongue, has a revelation, has an interpretation. Let all things be done for edification.

1 Corinthians 14:24–26

Spiritual Gifts in Scripture

Here are the scriptures where I have noticed the mention of spiritual gifts. This does not include Old Testament stories where God filled the gifted artisans to design His tabernacle or how He filled the judges from the Book of Judges or the kings of Israel with His Spirit so they could prophesy. Those stories are all over the Bible, and they affirm that spiritual gifts (just like baptism) are not just a New Testament truth. Spiritual gifts are a truth found in the entire Bible, from Genesis to Revelation![9] I have included the definitions of each spiritual gift as well. They are all working definitions. I hope a list of these gifts and their definitions point you in the right direction to discover your own spiritual gifts with the help of the Holy Spirit!

> **Scriptures:** *1 Corinthians 12–14; Ephesians 4:11–13; Romans 12:4–8; 1 Peter 4:10–11; Hebrews 2:4.*

Definitions:

Prophecy: supernatural real-time message from God to a person or people to provide growth, encouragement, and/or comfort.

Word of Knowledge: a word from the Holy Spirit that gives you information about a present or past event, something that the person telling you would otherwise never know.

Word of Wisdom: a word from the Holy Spirit that helps/connects with a present or future situation in your or someone else's life; something that gives you direction and guidance on how to move forward.

Exhortation: encouragement, comfort, console, provides sound wisdom in that needed moment.

Giving: freely shares what they have without expecting anything in return; cheerful in the process.

Leadership: manage, guides, oversees

Mercy: compassion and pity.

Helps: defend and support.

Administration: navigate, steer and guide.

Service/ministry: table service, waiting on others, hospitality, relieving, assisting, contributing.

Faith: confidence and certainty that what one believes will come to pass; full assurance.

Healing: the power to heal/repair; instantly or progressively.

Miracles: a powerful act that defies the laws of logic instantaneously.

Discerning of Spirits: supernaturally seeing/distinguishing the presence or activity of spirits demonic or heavenly.

Tongues: A prayer from the Holy Spirit spoken verbally in a language unknown to the person speaking it (supernaturally known, can be an actual language or one never heard of before)

Tongues Interpretation: interpreting the prayer that was spoken in tongues for the benefit of the church or gathering.

Apostle: someone who is first sent by God as a messenger of His heart. They pioneer the truth of God in unreached areas, build up the church of God, and advocate strongly for unity in the church. They desire to equip and release the body of believers into their callings and ministries. They have a deep love for the church.

Prophet: one who speaks for God and interprets His will to man regularly.

Evangelist: brings the good news and shares the Gospel regularly.

Pastor: shepherd and overseer of the local body of Christ.

Teacher: provides depth and clarity of God's Word.

God Still Speaks

I want to share with you a real-life example of a spiritual gift working in my life. That spiritual gift was a prophecy. *"For prophecy never came by the will of man, but holy men of God spoke as they were moved by the Holy Spirit"* (2 Peter 1:21).

It is vital that Jesus' followers function in spiritual gifts because they can literally change the trajectory of the recipient's life. In April 2019, I attended our church men's retreat. The first night at the retreat, our guest speaker, pastor Ben Dixon,[10] gave me a prophetic word in front of everyone. He said to me, "Daniel, what I see for you is write, write, write. I see you gathering materials together and providing a finished product that will help people." That first part of his prophecy was spot on because I was in the process of writing my first book, *The Weapons of Our Warfare: Living Victoriously in Jesus Christ*. I also like to draw, and God has used my artwork to speak into people's lives too. The "write, write, write" affirms the three books that God told me to write. This book *Unshakeable* is the second book, and I already have the third book in the works called *GRACE*.

But the next part of his prophecy really got to me. He continued by saying, "You had to put something on the shelf for a while. And you are wondering how you are going to recover from that. God will restore what you lost. God will still work through you." This hit home for me because my first child died in September 2018. I talked in detail about this story in my first book. I was devastated at the 2019 men's retreat, and I needed to hear that from God. After his message, I told our guest speaker my story with my first son Joseph. He told me to read Psalm 27. One verse stood out to me the most, and that verse from Psalm 27 was verse 4: *"One thing I have desired of the Lord, that will I seek: that I may dwell in the house of the Lord All the days of my life, to behold the beauty of the Lord, and to inquire in His temple."*

Blessing, I Will Bless You

When I got home from the retreat, that experience led me to a time of prayer with the LORD. I told Him, "Lord, You are my only desire. When hardships come my way, they take me from You. The loss of my first son and child has devastated me beyond measure. This trial almost made me walk away from You. But I didn't choose to follow You for what You could give me. I chose to follow You for who You are!" Then immediately in my spirit, I heard from the Holy Spirit, "Blessing, I will bless you!" I began to cry, and I replied, "You don't have to do that, LORD. That is not why I am seeking You. You don't owe me anything." Again, I heard, "Blessing, I will bless you!" I had no idea that those exact words came directly from Scripture.

> *Then the Angel of the Lord called to Abraham a second time out of heaven, and said: 'By Myself I have sworn, says the Lord, because you have done this thing, and have not withheld your son, your only son—blessing I will bless you, and multiplying I will multiply your descendants as the stars of the heaven and as the sand which is on the seashore; and your descendants shall possess the gate of their enemies. In your seed all the nations of the earth shall be blessed, because you have obeyed My voice.'*
>
> **Genesis 22:15–18**

I knew that God was talking about giving me another son after the loss of my first boy Joseph. The Holy Spirit told me to name my first boy Joseph because it means God will add and give increase. That promise was given to me in September 2018, when I was in the hospital room holding my first son. Now the Holy Spirit spoke to me again, seven months later, to reassure me of the promise He made to me regarding my second son.

Prophecy In a Coffee Shop

A few weeks after the men's retreat, my wife told me that she was pregnant for the second time. I was excited but also nervous; I didn't want to lose a child again. But God said He would provide. You can see this truth of His provision in the Genesis 22 story. And along the way, the Holy Spirit continued to affirm this prophecy of having another son. I had coffee with a couple from a local church, and they prayed for me, my wife, and my second son, who was in the womb at the time. The wife of the couple praying with me said, "I have a word from the Lord, and the word is: trouble will not come a second time!" Wow! I needed to hear that. A few months later, the Lord showed me in Scripture that what this lady spoke was not her own words; it was His Word! I was reading through the minor prophets and came across Nahum 1:9 (NIV), which says, *"Whatever they plot against the Lord, he will bring to an end; trouble will not come a second time."* I called this couple months later and asked, "Did you know what you prophesied was right from the Bible?" The wife responded, "I couldn't tell you the scriptural reference, but I knew it was in there somewhere!" The reason this means so much to me is because the Holy Spirit never contradicts Scripture! Also, if God says it, then it's a done deal (Numbers 23:19)!

Our Heavenly Father

In September/October of 2019, my wife was twenty-five weeks pregnant with our second son. This was the same age as our first boy Joseph when he died in the womb. I was at a church leaders conference in Texas, and my wife was at home. The Holy Spirit began to minister to me again and show me how I needed to trust God as a good Heavenly Father. The Holy Spirit told me that I struggled to do so because I did not have an example of a good earthly father in my life to show me this truth. But He said He was going to start bridging that gap of distrust with Father God because I wouldn't be able to fulfill the calling in my life unless I trusted God 100 percent. I told God that it would be difficult to trust Him if my second son died too. It's not that I didn't want to not trust God, but I was struggling. I didn't know how I would respond if this happened twice in a row. All I knew was that I needed a father in my life. My desire was for God to be that Father. Not that God owes me anything, but I cried out to Him, "Please God, help me to trust You. Please let me hold my living son!" Every night I would put my hands on my wife's womb and declare Psalm 118:17 over my second son, which says, *"I shall not die, but live, and declare the works of the Lord."* But I would insert my son's name "Elisha shall not die, but live, and declare the works of the Lord."

Our God Is Faithful

It was finally January 2020, and we had scheduled my wife to be induced for labor on January 9, 2020. On January 1, I checked in with the Lord again as we were getting closer to the delivery date. As I pressed in and cried out for protection over my son Elisha, the Holy Spirit said to me, "Last season, I needed you to hold My hand. This season I need you to hold your son." I once again began to weep. Because before the death of my first son, the Holy Spirit said to me, "Daniel, I need you to hold My hand." Isaiah 41:13 affirms this truth, *"For I, the Lord your God, will hold your right hand, saying to you, 'Fear not, I will help you.'"* On January 9, 2020, my second son Elisha was born! As I watched him take his first breath and come into this world, I was amazed and thankful at the goodness and splendor of God! The LORD is faithful! I'm going to say it again; the LORD is faithful! He is my restorer, and His word came to pass in my life! I pray His word also come to pass in yours!

A Double Portion

Even the name Elisha is prophetic. God gave my wife this name for our child, but when our first boy Joseph passed, it didn't seem to fit that part of our story. We waited for the promise of another child, and when God gave us our second boy, it made sense. Elijah was the mentor of Elisha. In 2 Kings 2, Elijah is about to be taken to heaven, and Elisha asks for a double portion of his anointing. Elijah says that's not up to him, but if God permits it, then it will be so. Elijah gets taken to heaven, and Elisha is left with his mantle and mission. Elisha gets the double portion, and while his mentor is taken to heaven, he stays on earth to fulfill his ministry. Do you see the picture here? My boy Joseph was taken, and my boy Elisha was given. God knew what He was doing with our boys, and He knew what He was doing with our story. Elisha means, "God is salvation." That's the foundation that

I had to stand on. When everything seemed to be taken from me, when the walls we built on that foundation of our faith fell, we still had Jesus (1 Corinthians 3:11)!

God Dream

I know I didn't talk about dream interpretation because I honestly don't know enough about it. As someone told me, "Preach what you know." But I have experienced dreams from God and have had them come true. I have included a picture at the end of this chapter that I drew. It comes from a dream God gave me years ago. The dream entailed my wife and me having a child. This dream came while we were dating, but before we were married and before we had children. In the dream, my wife was having complications during labor. The doctors called me and said they didn't know if mom and baby would make it. Then the dream skipped ahead, and both mom and baby were okay. I held our baby in my arms as my wife sat in the hospital bed. Everything was fine. My wife wanted me to tell her this dream often. Then God gave me the idea to draw it for her.

I drew this picture on December 22, 2017. I've titled it *God Dream.* I gave this picture to my wife as a Christmas present that year. Then we found out she was pregnant in April of 2018. We had been married for two years at that point. Our firstborn died in the womb, and I asked God, "What about the dream? You gave me this dream, and both Sonja and the baby were okay. What happened?" First Corinthians 13:9 says, "For we know in part, and we prophesy in part." That means that sometimes we won't understand the full meaning of a prophecy or dream. That is why we need to ask for the interpretation. God was giving me a heads up in this dream. Our first son's due date was scheduled for December 22, 2018. I drew the picture exactly one year before, on the same date before my wife was pregnant. My wife still had to give birth to our firstborn, and as soon as he came out of the womb, they handed him to me first. With our son Elisha, the doctors handed him to his mom first.

I held our firstborn exactly like the picture depicts. His head was resting on my left arm. Our son Joseph is okay because he is now held in the Father's arms. But the promise that I would hold another son was also depicted in this drawing. Since I received this dream before we were married, God was showing me in advance that I was to marry my now wife. He showed us that we would go through hardship, but because of the cross of Calvary, everything would be okay in the end. The dream God gave me did come true. I just didn't realize as I drew it that things would play out the way they did. Looking back now, I appreciate God speaking to me before all this happened. He spoke to me through a dream.

Dreams and interpretation of dreams are part of the major list of other spiritual gifts in the Bible. Yet, there are even more spiritual gifts available to us. My heart is that you will discover which spiritual gifts you have and then use them. You never know who needs the spiritual gift that God has given you.

A true Jesus follower functions in spiritual gifts!

THE
HEALING

CHAPTER SEVEN
RESTORED RELATIONSHIPS

A true Jesus follower restores broken relationships!

In Genesis 41, we see that Joseph interpreted Pharaoh's dreams. Both dreams pointed to the same outcome; there would be a severe famine in the land. There would be seven years of plentiful harvest, and then there would be seven years of no grain at all. Joseph suggested to Pharaoh that he put someone in charge of the grain, that they would gather all the grain in the plentiful years and then distribute the grain during the years of famine. Pharaoh thought this to be a great idea, and he put Joseph in charge. Joseph got out of prison and became second in command in all of Egypt! At the age of thirty years old, Joseph was promoted (Genesis 41:46)! It was thirteen years later that God fulfilled His promise to Joseph (Genesis 37:2). All the countries had to come to Joseph to buy grain for their families (Genesis 41:57). That included Joseph's brothers, which was now the second part of Joseph's dream coming to pass; that his brothers would come and bow down to him (Genesis 42:6).

Joseph was about thirty-seven to thirty-nine years old when he first saw his brothers again. Genesis 45:11 states that there were five years left of famine. The seven years of plenty had already passed. Joseph's brothers went to him during the years of famine. Later in the story, Joseph dismisses his brothers to go get his brother Benjamin, his father Jacob, and the rest of his family, to bring them to Egypt. Since Joseph started serving Pharaoh at thirty years old, he would have been thirty-nine years old at the time he saw his brothers again. By the time Joseph would see his dad again, he would be close to forty years old. That was the third part of his dream being fulfilled, where his moms and dad would also come to bow to him (Genesis 37:10). This meant that nearly twenty-three years had passed before he saw his dad and nearly twenty years since he saw his brothers! The full fulfillment of Joseph's dream came to pass over two decades later! But now Joseph meets with his ten half-brothers for the first time in a long time. He was seventeen years old the last time he saw them.

God Promotes

Before I continue with the focus of this chapter, I want to acknowledge Joseph's promotion. I didn't feel led by the Spirit to dedicate an entire chapter on Joseph being promoted. The reason behind that is because I am still in the waiting process for the entire fulfillment of my God dream. I remember walking up to the campus of my community college, and I saw a new church building being built. As I looked at the work being done, this desire stirred in my heart, "I am going to lead a church one day." This desire came from the Lord, as it says in 1 Corinthians 12:18, "But now God has set the members, each one of them, in the body just as He pleased."

The first position of pastoring that I took on was

being the youth pastor at my church. Then I simultaneously pastored the young adults of our church. I youth pastored from May 2013 to January 2019. I pastored the young adults from January 2015 to the present. In September of 2020, I became the men's pastor of our church, and I also became the associate pastor. Just like Joseph, I was thirty years old when I became second in command. I love being where I am right now in my pastoral call. Yet, I know what God has for me in the end. God has been preparing me and training me this entire time. Getting me fully ready for what He has planned for my future. That is why this story of Joseph is so encouraging to me. God has already fulfilled His promise to me to be in ministry the way that I am today. He has brought me further than I ever thought I would go. I didn't want to dismiss this promotion part because you may be waiting for yours, or you may have already experienced your full promotion. Though I won't dedicate a chapter to this truth, I want you to know that God promotes! It can't be earned. It's freely given. We simply believe Him and receive where He places us. God has a promotion for each one of us!

"For promotion cometh neither from the east, nor from the west, nor from the south. But God is the judge: he putteth down one, and setteth up another" (Psalm 75:6–7, KJV).

Genesis 42–45 has a lot of material to be discussed. I will not be able to explain everything from these chapters. I want to focus on how Joseph interacted with his brothers, who treated him so badly. Instead of writing his brothers off, Joseph chose to reconcile with his brothers. Yes, he had a few moments of frustration, and yes, he had a few moments where he toyed around with them. Instead of paying them back for what they did to him, Joseph made a conscious decision to restore his relationship with his brothers. I'm going to walk us through the next few chapters and touch on the aspects that relate to Joseph restoring his relationship with his brothers. The process he uses is an example for us today.

> *So Joseph's ten brothers went down to buy grain in Egypt.*
> *Joseph saw his brothers and recognized them, but he acted as a stranger to them and spoke roughly to them. Then he said to them, 'Where do you come from?...so Joseph recognized his brothers, but they did not recognize him.'*
> *So he put them all together in prison for three days.*

Genesis 42:3,7–8,17

This Is Painful

Joseph is upset when he first sees his brothers. Think about all they did to him. He could have had them killed on the spot! His brothers wouldn't have recognized him because the Egyptians looked much different than the Israelites. Joseph was clean-shaven on his head and face. That alone would have made him look much different than his brothers, whose faces were covered with beards. Instead of killing them, he spoke roughly to them and had them put in prison. They put him in a pit, so putting them in prison for three days seemed fair to him. I could only imagine the heartache that Joseph was going through as he saw his brothers. Two decades had passed, he is second in command in all of Egypt, and he holds all ten of his half-brothers' lives in his very hands.

The brothers that wanted to kill him but then sold him are now in his midst, asking him for help. How would you have responded if you were Joseph?

Joseph then tells one of his ten brothers to go and get their youngest brother, which is Benjamin. Benjamin stayed home because his father, Jacob, didn't want to send him. Jacob didn't want to send all his kids and have something happen to all of them and then have no more sons. Jacob already thought Joseph was dead, and he couldn't bear to lose Benjamin as well, since Joseph and Benjamin were both from Rachel, whom Jacob loved. Joseph wants to see his full brother Benjamin. So, he suggests that one brother stays in prison while the other nine brothers go back home with the grain. They would then convince their dad to bring Benjamin with them the next time they needed grain. So, Joseph keeps Simeon in prison (v.24). But look at the brother's response in verse Genesis 42:21, *"Then they said to one another, 'We are truly guilty concerning our brother, for we saw the anguish of his soul when he pleaded with us, and we would not hear; therefore this distress has come upon us.'"* The brothers knew what they did was wrong. They truly thought that their brother had died (Genesis 42:13). But there wasn't much they could do to fix that. We might not always get an apology from those who hurt us, but it helps when we do.

Restoration Is Possible

In my first book, I talked extensively about my relationship with my dad.[11] But soon before I published my first book, I had an encounter with my dad that I couldn't write about until now. I remember sitting in the car with my dad just three months after my first son Joseph died. My dad told me how my sister told him the news, and he was devastated for me. He told me how he had never experienced anything like that and how he didn't know how he would handle it if he did. As I sat with my dad in my car, I had a choice to make. I could let all the hurt that has happened between us stop me from engaging in this conversation with him, or I could focus on the moment and let him be my dad. My heart was open, and I chose to not focus on the past but to embrace the moment.

My dad began to share more of his heart with me and explain how sorry he was for not keeping his promises to me as a kid. He apologized for never taking me fishing, hunting, camping, etc. He knew the consequences of breaking those promises and how the ultimate consequence was that he didn't get to be in my life like he had hoped. I was twenty-eight years old when I sat in the car with him that day. He couldn't believe how much of my life he had missed. I was eleven years old when my parents divorced. Nearly seventeen years later, we had this moment together, just like Joseph and his brothers. While my dad wasn't with me in the hospital room holding me as I held my son Joseph, my dad was with me in the car three months later, having a genuine conversation with me. In that moment, I was simply grateful that for the first time in a long time, I was able to have a moment like that with my dad. My dad missed a lot of my life, but he was there for me in a moment where I needed him most. That conversation with my dad took place on New Year's Eve of 2018. That was the last deep conversation I have had with him. The question then is this: are you willing to restore relationships with those who hurt you the most? It doesn't come easy, but it needs to be done. Let's continue to see how Joseph interacted with his brothers as he had to deal with twenty years of separation from them.

> *And he (Joseph) turned himself away from them and wept...Then Joseph gave a command to fill their sacks with grain, to restore_every man's money to his sack, and to give them provisions for the journey. Thus he did for them. So they loaded their donkeys with the grain and departed from there. But as one of them opened his sack to give his donkey feed at the encampment, he saw his money; and there it was, in the mouth of his sack. So he said to his brothers, 'My money has been restored, and there it is, in my sack!' Then their hearts failed them and they were afraid, saying to one another, 'What is this that God has done to us?'*

Genesis 42:24–28

At first glance, it seems that Joseph's brothers have been set up. They are afraid that it looks like they stole the grain, even though they truly paid for it. They were already feeling guilty about what they had done to their brother, and they felt that they deserved nothing but hardship as a result. To have their money returned to them displayed Joseph's heart towards his brothers; they owed him nothing. His brothers didn't know that the second in rank was Joseph. They wouldn't think this was a blessing but rather a curse. Once they got home to their father Jacob, they soon realized that each one had received their money back in full (Genesis 42:35)! It's interesting that they asked this question, "What is this that God has done to us?" Before we can restore relationships with others, we need to know that we have been restored in our relationship with God.

Restoration Is Necessary

Our church goes out daily and shares the gospel with people. We use a tool called "Jesus at the Door." It is an effective tool created by evangelist Scott McNamara.[12] It is the Gospel, and that is why it has power in it (Romans 1:16–17)! Our church has adopted his style of evangelism because it is effective and gives people a chance to not only hear the Gospel but to respond to it in that moment. As we were witnessing one day, I began to get convicted. I am out partnering with the Holy Spirit, who is restoring the relationship between God and people, but I have not restored relationships with people I know I should have. So, I made a list of the brothers and sisters in Christ with which I needed to restore relationships. With one individual, I sat down and talked with them for over three hours! I sat back and listened to all the ways I had hurt them by things I said or did. My intention was not to hurt them. There was simply a misunderstanding because of miscommunication on my end. But I sat and listened to them regardless because it was what they needed from me. My flesh didn't want any part of that. But I knew in my spirit that restoring this relationship meant that I was obeying God. God matters to me first, but I also don't want to be at odds with anyone, especially if I can help it (Romans 12:18).

> Now all things are of God, who has reconciled us to Himself through Jesus Christ, and has given us the ministry of reconciliation, that is, that God was in Christ reconciling the world to Himself, not imputing their trespasses to them, and has committed to us the word of reconciliation. Now then, we are ambassadors for Christ, as though

God were pleading through us: we implore you on Christ's behalf, be reconciled to God. For He made Him who knew no sin to be sin for us, that we might become the righteousness of God in Him.

2 Corinthians 5:18–21

This is one of my most motivating passages for evangelism. That word, reconcile,[13] means to change a person from hostility to friendship. To exchange what you are currently holding on to for something else, something better. We have to understand that God has reconciled and restored our relationship with us. He exchanged His anger towards our sin for the right relationship with us forever. It came at a price. It cost Jesus His life. By the blood of Jesus alone, we have been brought near to God again (Ephesians 2:13). We didn't have to earn our way back to God. We didn't have to beg and plead our way back to God. We simply confess our sin, repent from our actions, and let the sacrifice of Jesus be our source of restoration with God (1 John 1:9). If God says that is good enough for our relationship with Him to be restored, then why would we hold a different standard for others? Please take a moment and read Matthew 18:21–35 in your Bible.

God Forgave Us of an Immeasurable Amount of Debt!

When we go out and share the Gospel using the "Jesus at the Door" approach, one of the questions we ask people is this: "Let's say your debt with God represented $10,000 you owed the bank. If you didn't have the money to pay it, but I did, and I gave you $10,000 to pay off your debt, then what would happen to it?" The obvious answer is, it would be gone. We continue by saying, "And that's exactly what Jesus did for you on the cross. He wrote you a check, signed in His blood, and He is standing at the door of your heart today, wanting you to cash it in." Have you allowed Jesus to pay your debt with God? My sins totaled more than $10,000 that I would owe God. I owed God a debt that I couldn't pay, and Jesus paid that debt for me. So wouldn't the correct response on my end be that I would also release people of the debt that they "owe me?" (Ephesians 4:32).

Restoration Requires a New Heart

Restoration of relationships begins with having a heart for people. This doesn't always mean that we feel like forgiving them or restoring relationships with them. But the Lord has really been ministering to me about feelings and love through my second son Elisha. As I am writing this book, my son is almost two years old. He has already tested my patience on multiple occasions. But when he wants something to drink, I give it to him. When he wants to eat, I feed him. When he wants to take a nap, I hold him. Even now, as he just smeared his yogurt all over the table instead of eating it, I took the time to wipe his face off and clean up after him. How I treat my son is not always based on my feelings. It's not even based on a mere sense of responsibility. I take care of my son because he is my son. The Lord showed me this about Himself. He ministered to my heart this morning, "Daniel, if you take care of your son regardless of how you feel, then it's the same with Me. I am here for you regardless of how I feel." Now, this meant a lot to me this morning because sometimes I feel like I can't go to God and spend time with Him. Sometimes I think He is upset with me, or I did something wrong, so I can't come to Him in prayer or in reading the Bible. But God doesn't allow His feelings to dictate His faithfulness (2 Timothy 2:13). I take care of my son because he is my son, and I love him. God takes care of me because I am one of His sons, and He loves me. God takes care of you because He loves you, and you belong to Him!

So, I have a few questions for you. Do you have a heart for people? Do you allow your feelings to dictate your faithfulness towards God? Do you allow your feelings to dictate your interactions with others? What makes you continue to provide for your children when they have caused you a lot of pain before? What makes you continue to be there for your spouse when they have probably caused you a lot of pain? Why do you give forgiveness to them and not to others? Because you love them. The love you have for them overrides how you feel towards them (1 Peter 4:8). Love is an emotion, but it is also an action (1 Corinthians 13). We need to exhibit love not only for those closest to us but also for the stranger and for those who have hurt us. Another question is, do you really hate that person so much that you are not willing to restore your relationship with them?

> If someone says, 'I love God,' and hates his brother, he is a liar; for he who does not love his brother whom he has seen, how can he love God whom he has not seen? And this commandment we have from Him: that he who loves God must love his brother also.
>
> **1 John 4:20–21**

If anyone had a good reason to not forgive and hold a grudge, it would be Joseph. His brothers hated him, almost killed him, sold him as a slave, separated him from his dad. All of this happened when he was only seventeen years old. As a result of being in a foreign land, he worked as a slave with an entire nation that he didn't even know, was falsely accused of adultery, and was put in prison and forgotten in prison. Yes, Joseph was blessed by God and moved to second in rank in the land, and he also was blessed to get married and have two children. All of that came at a cost (Genesis 41:50–52). When Joseph was reunited with his brothers after twenty years, he responded by having a heart for his family. He didn't respond in hatred. Is your heart really that hard towards a person that you refuse to restore your relationship with them?

They might have done something to you that brings you to tears if you even think about it, let alone speak about it. I am not undermining the horrors and evils that have been done to you or those around you. I am not saying that what was done to you is okay and that it doesn't matter. That person will stand before God one day and give an account of their lives, and they will have to explain to God why they did what they did to you (Hebrews 9:27; 2 Corinthians 5:10). What I am encouraging you to do, is to think about all the evils you have done towards God. Have you ever broken God's heart, lied to Him, cheated on Him, cursed at Him, turned away from Him, ignored Him, rejected Him, etc. And how did God respond to you? If you answered no to all of these, then you are not being honest (1 John 1:8). Whether your sin towards God was big or small, we have all done something to break His heart (Romans 3:23). Yet God did not respond towards us with hatred, but He responded to us with a heart for restoration.

So the men took that present and Benjamin, and they took double money in their hand, and arose and went down to Egypt; and they stood before Joseph. When Joseph saw Benjamin with them, he said to the steward of his house, 'Take these men to my home, and slaughter an animal and make ready; for these men will dine with me at noon.' Then the man did as Joseph ordered, and the man brought the men into Joseph's house. Now the men were afraid because they were brought into Joseph's house; and they said, 'It is because of the money, which was returned in our sacks the first time, that we are brought in, so that he may make a case against us and seize us, to take us as slaves with our donkeys.' When they drew near to the steward of Joseph's house, they talked with him at the door of the house, and said, 'O sir, we indeed came down the first time to buy food; but it happened, when we came to the encampment, that we opened our sacks, and there, each man's money was in the mouth of his sack, our money in full weight; so we have brought it back in our hand. And we have brought down other money in our hands to buy food. We do not know who put our money in our sacks.'
But he said, 'Peace be with you, do not be afraid. Your God and the God of your father has given you treasure in your sacks; I had your money.' Then he brought Simeon out to them. So the man brought the men into Joseph's house and gave them water, and they washed their feet; and he gave their donkeys feed. Then they made the present ready for Joseph's coming at noon, for

*they heard that they would eat bread there. And
when Joseph came home, they brought him the
present which was in their hand into the house,
and bowed down before him to the earth. Then he
asked them about their well-being, and said, 'Is
your father well, the old man of whom you spoke?
Is he still alive?'*

Genesis 43:15–27

You Don't Need to Knock

Joseph doesn't keep his brothers at the door, but
he invites them into his home. How many people are you
keeping at a distance when God is asking you to pull them
close? The gospel of God is written all throughout this story,
but especially here in Genesis 43. An animal was slaughtered,
their feet were washed, their money was returned to them,
and they sat together in a home. This is a picture of how
God treats us. His Son was slain for us; He has washed
us clean, He doesn't make us stand outside, He invites us
into His heavenly home. God desires restoration with us!
Joseph demonstrates God's heart towards his brothers as He
knows that God demonstrates this same heart towards him
(Romans 5:8). You might ask, "How can you expect me to
love someone to this extent when they have hurt me so bad?
Do you really expect me to have that person in my home?"
Please take a moment and read Luke 7:36–50 in your Bible.

Do you relate more to the Pharisee sitting at the table
or the woman lying on the floor? Depending on your answer,
this will determine your drive towards restoring your broken
relationships. You have to use wisdom and listen to the
guidance of the Holy Spirit in your life when it comes to

restoring relationships with those who hurt you. There might be some people that you are not meant to be around, and that doesn't necessarily mean that you haven't forgiven them and restored that relationship with them in your heart. But my question to you would be, according to all the Scripture you just read above, is that current relationship past restoration? With all the Scripture you just read, do you still feel in your heart not to let that person in your home? Then let God be the judge between you and that person. All I know is that if I truly follow Jesus, then I need to seek reconciliation with as many people as possible.

Finally Set Free

> *Then Joseph could not restrain himself before all those who stood by him, and he cried out, 'Make everyone go out from me!' So no one stood with him while Joseph made himself known to his brothers. And he wept aloud, and the Egyptians and the house of Pharaoh heard it. Then Joseph said to his brothers, 'I am Joseph; does my father still live?' But his brothers could not answer him, for they were dismayed in his presence. And Joseph said to his brothers, 'Please come near to me.' So they came near. Then he said: 'I am Joseph your brother, whom you sold into Egypt.' Then he fell on his brother Benjamin's neck and wept, and Benjamin wept on his neck. Moreover he kissed all his brothers and wept over them, and after that his brothers talked with him.*

Genesis 45:1–4, 14–15

A true Jesus follower restores broken relationships!

CHAPTER EIGHT
GOD SENT

*A true Jesus follower is sent by God
so others can be saved!*

> *But now, do not therefore be grieved or angry
> with yourselves because you sold me here; for
> God sent me before you to preserve life...And
> God sent me before you to preserve a posterity
> for you in the earth, and to save your lives by a
> great deliverance. So now it was not you who sent
> me here, but God; and He has made me a father
> to Pharaoh, and lord of all his house, and a ruler
> throughout all the land of Egypt.*

Genesis 45:5–8

Joseph received more than just a dream from God. It
wasn't just a dream about him lording over his brothers and
parents. In Genesis 45–49, we see that Joseph's dream fully
comes true! His brothers go back to their father and let Jacob
know that Joseph is alive. Pharaoh hears about Joseph's
brothers coming to visit him, and Pharaoh tells Joseph to
send for his entire family from Canaan and to bring them to
Egypt. Pharaoh provides a place for them to live. Joseph sees
his father again. Jacob meets Joseph's two sons and blesses
them. And the entire nation of Israel is saved because God
sent Joseph ahead of them! Seventy people in Israel's family

multiplied into two to three million people over the course of 400 years. We see this in the Book of Exodus, where God then delivers Israel from their slavery. But Joseph didn't just save his family from a food famine. He saved them and many others from much more than that.

Life Is Not that Simple

I remember having lunch with my older brother in Southern California. The restaurant we ate at was right on the beach. It had a beautiful view and amazing food! As we sat and talked with our family, I began to look out at the beach, and I started to "people watch." I saw people fishing off the dock, tanning on the beach, riding on bikes, and playing volleyball on the sand. I desired to be out there with those people, enjoying life as if everything was normal. But I knew that life was not that simple. Knowing that all people will live eternal life in heaven or hell changes my entire perspective on life. I can't live normally anymore. My eyes have been opened. I know the truth.

> *Do not love the world or the things in the world.*
> *If anyone loves the world, the love of the Father*
> *is not in him. For all that is in the world—the lust*
> *of the flesh, the lust of the eyes, and the pride of*
> *life—is not of the Father but is of the world. And*
> *the world is passing away, and the lust of it; but*
> *he who does the will of God abides forever.*

1 John 2:15–17

As a result of our sin, the earth is going to end (Romans 5:12). God is going to create a new heaven and new earth (Revelation 21–22). The earth and the life we live now will one day be no more. God is angry at sin, and there is wrath to come. We see this truth revealed in Romans 1:18–23. Please take a moment to read it in your Bible. We have a choice to make. We can choose to get to know God for who He is, or we can ignore Him. Pleading ignorance on judgment day is not a valid answer. My Bible college professor introduced me to the three C's. He said, "God has revealed His truth to us; through Creation, our Conscience and other Christians." What he was trying to tell us was that there is plenty of evidence to know that God exists. I don't want to make God angry, and I don't want to be at odds with God. So, what do we do? We respond to His Gospel.

> *For I am not ashamed of the gospel of Christ, for it is the power of God to salvation for everyone who believes, for the Jew first and also for the Greek. For in it the righteousness of God is revealed from faith to faith; as it is written, 'The just shall live by faith.'*

Romans 1:16–17

The Good News

God tells us that His standard is righteousness. Righteousness means to be put into right relationship with God.[14] For man to be in right relationship with God, they would have to be perfect like God. But the Bible says that no man is righteous (Romans 3:10). God gave man a law that if we could live by it, we would be deemed perfect. In the Old Testament Jewish law, there were over 400 commandments. We couldn't even obey one command from God in the very beginning (Genesis 2:17); what makes you think man is capable of obeying over 400 commands? The point was not for us to achieve perfection through the law God gave. The point of the law was for us to realize that we can't live perfectly, and we, therefore, need saving. We need help from God. God is a loving God (1 John 4:8), and He is also a just God (Isaiah 30:18). Though His heart yearns to be back in relationship with us after we say sorry for our mistakes, He still has to deal with the sin problem. He can't just neglect it and act like it never happened. There are consequences for our sin. When we sin, we are against God. If sin dwells in us, we can't be on His side. For sin separates us from Him (Isaiah 59:2).

He Needed a Man to Fulfill the Law

> *For the law, having a shadow of the good things to come, and not the very image of the things, can never with these same sacrifices, which they offer continually year by year, make those who approach perfect. For then would they not have ceased to be offered? For the worshipers, once purified, would have had no more consciousness of sins. But in those sacrifices there is a reminder of sins every year. For it is not possible that the blood of bulls and goats could take away sins.*

Hebrews 10:1–4

From the very beginning, even with Adam and Eve, we see that animal sacrifices were instituted on behalf of sin. Genesis 3:21 says, *"Also for Adam and his wife the Lord God made tunics of skin, and clothed them."*

So, God sent Jesus, fully God but also fully man. This God-man fulfilled the requirements of the law towards man. Jesus' final work on the cross was completed when He said,

"It is finished." No longer were we bound by the works of the law for salvation. Jesus didn't sin once either.

> *Seeing then that we have a great High Priest who has passed through the heavens, Jesus the Son of God, let us hold fast our confession. For we do not have a High Priest who cannot sympathize with our weaknesses, but was in all points tempted as we are, yet without sin.*

Hebrews 4:14–15

This qualified Him to be the proper sacrifice for sinners. If Jesus was a sinner, then He couldn't cancel out other sinners' debts. Being conceived of the Holy Spirit allowed Him to be untouched by sin. Because we know from Psalm 51:5 that every man born into this world is born into sin. But God can't be affected by sin (James 1:13). That's why it is so important for us to know that Jesus is God. Only God qualified for this sacrifice. No other man could have done what He did!

But Jesus also was a man. We have to believe that too because the debt of man had to be paid by a man. Now that Jesus fulfilled the law as a man for man, man still had to pay the penalty of sin. Not only did Jesus live the perfect life that we couldn't live, but He paid the price we should have paid! Jesus died in our place on behalf of our sin. Then Jesus rose from the dead three days later, and all the sin that He took on Himself stayed in the grave while He rose anew to heaven. When we put faith in God that what He did was sufficient for our salvation, then we, too, when we die, will go be with God in heaven. Sin won't separate us from God anymore. Not because of what we did, but because of what He has done on that cross (Colossians 2:14)! Therefore, the fear of death (being separated from God for all eternity) no longer binds us. We don't have to worry about being separated from Him any longer!

> *Inasmuch then as the children have partaken of flesh and blood, He Himself likewise shared in the same, that through death He might destroy him who had the power of death, that is, the devil, and release those who through fear of death were all their lifetime subject to bondage.*

Hebrews 2:14–15

Saved by His Grace

We can't work our way into heaven. How much good work must someone do to be in right relationship with a perfect God? We can't work our way out of our debt. Our debt is too much for us to pay. Our debt must be forgiven, and God alone has the power to forgive sins (Mark 2:7). God says He forgives sins by the blood and sacrifice of His Son, not by our good works (Ephesians 2:8–9). Good works are important as we are called to do works worthy of repentance (Matthew 3:8). But we don't do good works to be saved. We are saved, so we do good works!

The good news from God is, *"For He made Him (Jesus) who knew no sin to be sin for us, that we might become the righteousness of God in Him"* (2 Corinthians 5:21). God wants us to put our faith in Jesus because Jesus gets us right with God! God doesn't want us separated from Him; He wants us close to Him. 1 Timothy 2:3–4 says, *"For this is good and acceptable in the sight of God our Savior, who desires all men to be saved and to come to the knowledge of the truth.*" God's desire to be close to us can be found in Ezekiel 18. Please take a moment to read it in your Bible. God's promise for eternal life with Him is available and true (Titus 1:2).

God Sends People

God sent people to proclaim this message of salvation. God gave His creation a promise from the very beginning. Genesis 3:15 says, *"And I will put enmity between you and the woman, and between your seed and her Seed; He shall bruise your head, and you shall bruise His heel."* God promised a solution for man's sin. He promised a Savior! He entrusted this promise to many people (Acts 7). He promised that He would send a Savior because we simply can't save ourselves. God preserved His promise and then fulfilled His promise by having Jesus being born, dying, and rising to life again! Each person that God sent had a choice to make; will I continue living simply like the rest of the world, or will I respond to the gospel and share it with others so they can be saved?

Joseph played a role in our salvation. He didn't quit nor give up along the way. Our salvation was able to happen simply because Joseph didn't waver from God's dream and call on his life. Hear me out. We can only go to heaven through faith in Jesus Christ. Jesus is the only name by which we can be saved (Acts 4:12; John 14:6). But while Joseph's brothers were concerned about their day-to-day lives, Joseph knew something was bigger at play in his life after he had received that dream from God. Joseph's obedience saved many lives. By Joseph giving up his life, he didn't just save his family; it saved the billions of believers' lives that would come to faith in Jesus afterward. God worked through Abraham, Isaac, and Jacob to bring about the Savior (Jesus Christ). Then the promise came to Joseph's life, and generation and God asked Joseph the same thing He asks us today; are you willing to lay down your life so others can be saved? Are you willing to give up your life so that others can find theirs? This is the heart of God (John 15:13).

Philippians 2 tells us that Jesus came down, leaving the majesty of heaven for His own creation. Jesus was sent on our behalf (Romans 8:3). We are called to be like Jesus; therefore, we must walk as He walked and be willing to be God-sent like Him and Joseph (1 Peter 2:21).

> *Then Jesus said to His disciples, "If anyone desires to come after Me, let him deny himself, and take up his cross, and follow Me. For whoever desires to save his life will lose it, but whoever loses his life for My sake will find it. For what profit is it to a man if he gains the whole world, and loses his own soul? Or what will a man give in exchange for his soul?*

Matthew 16:24–26

Jesus Satisfies

When we hit the streets to share the Gospel, "Jesus at the Door" style, people encounter Jesus! Through the Holy Spirit, they tangibly feel His presence. When we pray for people, we ask them if they felt anything as we prayed. We get responses like warmth, love, joy, kindness, hope, and much more. During one of our outreaches, I crossed paths with a teenage couple on their way to eat lunch. I prayed for the boy, and he said, "I am not hungry anymore. That is the weirdest thing. I seriously am not hungry anymore!" His girlfriend looked at him awkwardly. I didn't know what to say until the Holy Spirit brought this verse to my mind: John 6:35 *"And Jesus said to them, 'I am the bread of life. He who comes to Me shall never hunger, and he who believes in Me shall never thirst.'"* I explained to the young man that after he eats food, he would be hungry again. But Jesus satisfies his true hunger; to know God and be known by Him (John 17:3). We ask if they feel anything to invoke a response. Those encounters by the Holy Spirit that they experience raise their faith to believe that Jesus is there with them. As we give the invitation, we see many people say yes to follow Jesus!

But we also get responses that surprise me. People say things like, "I am in school and don't have time." Or "I work a lot and can't commit to church right now." Or "I will think about it. Maybe later." "What will a man give in exchange for his soul?" They don't realize that what they are holding on to in this life is about to cost them everything. In these one hundred years of life, what could be more valuable to us than living with God for eternity? How are people not willing to exchange one hundred years of pleasure in this life for an infinite number of years with God in heaven forever? (Hebrews 11:24–26). If we keep living like everyone else, then not only will we fall into the same trap as them, but others will never have the chance to hear the truth (John 14:6). It's not easy being the messenger to a world that chooses the creature over the Creator (Romans 1:25). But when God marks you and sends you, it's for the purpose that others can be saved. Someone has to share the message. We are not responsible for the results, but we are responsible for proclaiming the message (John 3:16–17).

Are You Willing?

With all this truth in mind, I realized that I was not going to be able to live a carefree life like everyone else. While people enjoy their day-to-day activities, I know that I am sent by God to live differently than everyone else around me. I am not saying that living for God is a buzzkill. Psalm 16:11 says, *"You will show me the path of life; In Your presence is fullness of joy; At Your right hand are pleasures forevermore."* I truly enjoy playing basketball, playing with my son, having date nights with my wife, watching a good movie, etc. But living for God does require sacrifice. There will be a day when God judges the earth (Acts 17:31; 2 Corinthians 5:10). Knowing this truth, how am I going to choose to live my life? My desire now is to partner with God and live a life that brings people into a relationship with God. Even if it means that I "miss out" on certain earthly activities. Because eternity is a long time. Please take a moment to read 1 Peter 4:1–5 in your Bible.

God's Will Not Mine

I remember sitting in one of my Bible college classes, and my professor was discussing the topic of spiritual gifts. He used the gift of the pastor as an example, and he said, "If God has called you to be a pastor, then why are you spending so much time playing basketball?" He said this generally to the class, but I knew God was speaking through him to me. So I chose not to play basketball my senior year. My friends didn't understand it. But a former basketball player from my college told me this when I first enrolled at Multnomah, "Daniel, there is more to life than playing basketball." As a result of not playing basketball during my senior year, I had time to become the new youth pastor at my church. That platform was God's will for me to reach as many people as possible with the Gospel. But I couldn't do that when I had a basketball in my hand seven days a week. Don't get me wrong; God can work through sports to give Him glory. Sports just wasn't the main platform that He chose to work through me on. I don't regret my decision for a second.

I still play basketball for fun now, but I play with a different focus. Win or lose, I try to take every opportunity on that court to point people to Jesus. God gave me the ability to play basketball, and it brings joy to His heart to watch me play. It relieves my stress, and it brings me great joy to run for hours, putting a simple ball into a metal rim, over and over and over again. Yet I would give that all up for Him because I know what I am sent to do. I am not alone in this either. Some of my former youth gave up their sports careers of football and soccer to focus more on winning souls with Jesus (Proverbs 11:30). One of them quit their sports career their senior year too. We can enjoy the good things that God has given us, but it does require sacrifice to be sent by Him.

Are you willing to be sent by God so others can be saved? Are you ready to lose your life, so others can find theirs? So often, we want God to work through us and use us for His purpose and glory. But are we truly willing to pay the price? Do we know that being sent by God requires a full denial of oneself? Are we willing to be used by God even if hardship lies before us? When we understand His plan to save man, then yes, we will gladly want to be sent by God!

Diving Deeper

> *Moreover He called for a famine in the land; He*
> *destroyed all the provision of bread. He sent a*
> *man before them—Joseph—who was sold as*
> *a slave. They hurt his feet with fetters, He was*
> *laid in irons. Until the time that his word came to*
> *pass, The word of the Lord tested him.*

Psalm 105:16–19

We acquire more clarity about Joseph's story from this Psalm. Let's unpack each of these truths: God cursed the land, God sent a man, and God tested him.

We Are Blessed, The Earth Is Cursed

Notice that God was the one who called for a famine in the land. A famine didn't just appear out of nowhere. God orchestrated it. But why? Why did there have to be a famine at all? This famine reminds me of the curse that God put on the earth at the beginning of creation. After Adam and Eve sinned, God cursed the earth.

> *Then to Adam He said, 'Because you have heeded*
> *the voice of your wife, and have eaten from the*
> *tree of which I commanded you, saying, 'You*
> *shall not eat of it:' Cursed is the ground for your*
> *sake; In toil you shall eat of it all the days of your*
> *life. Both thorns and thistles it shall bring forth*
> *for you, and you shall eat the herb of the field. In*
> *the sweat of your face you shall eat bread till you*
> *return to the ground, for out of it you were taken;*
> *For dust you are, and to dust you shall return.'*

Genesis 3:17–19

The curse of the earth, just like the famine in the land, was meant to help us, not hurt us. Without there being a struggle in the land, there would be no need for us to seek God. Just like the bronze serpent in Numbers 21, God wants us to look up at Him! Look up and be saved! God didn't curse Adam and Eve; He blessed them (Genesis 1:28). God didn't famish Israel (Jacob); He famished the land so that His people would seek Him out. God loves His creation. He doesn't want to harm it. But if God has to harm the ground to save man, then He will do it. People are God's most prized possession. The Bible itself says that even the angels don't get a second chance at salvation (2 Peter 2:4). Even many animals had to be sacrificed in the Old Testament system (Leviticus) because of man's sin. God loves the earth, animals, and angels, but He loves His people the most. Even when the fallen state of man in Genesis 6 moved God to destroy all mankind (Noah and His family were spared), it hurt God's heart so much. He swore He wouldn't flood the earth ever again.

Being Sent Requires Sacrifice

Why does being sent require sacrifice? Why can't we continue living the way we are living and still proclaim His Gospel message. I remember being newly saved and going to a friend's bachelor party. I never struggled with drinking alcohol. But I did have an addictive personality. Before we left the house and throughout the night, I drank a lot. I was not out of control, but it was past the point of an alcohol buzz. As we bar hopped, I saw one of my brother's friends. We said hi to each other and talked for a second as we hadn't seen each other in a while. Then he asked me this question,

"What are you doing here?" He continued, "Last I heard, you were going to school to be a pastor. So, what are you doing here drinking at a bar?" I was immediately convicted. He wasn't talking about me being present at a bar as we know Jesus sat at the table with sinners (Matthew 9:10). What he was really asking me was, "Why was I acting like everyone else when I am sent by God to be different?" I went home that night and repented for my sin. I asked God to forgive me and help me to never do that again (1 John 1:9). Being sent by God will cost you. Are you willing to give up your earthly pleasures for others to come to know Jesus?

Tested Not Tempted

You will be tested when you are sent. I've heard mature believers in Christ say that God will never test you, but He will allow it. We tiptoe around this situation simply because it makes us uncomfortable to think of God doing such a thing. It really goes back to how our earthly fathers treated us. We tend to view our Heavenly Father the way we view our earthly father. Alternatively, it could go back to those in authority over us and the fact that they abused their authority. But we need to remember that God is perfect and just and wouldn't abuse His sovereign authority over us (Deuteronomy 32:4). God is not our earthly father, and He is not the person who hurt us. He does not pervert His authority towards us even though He is Lord over us. His correction is perfect, and when He tests us, it is meant for us to prevail, not to fail. In Genesis 22:1, it says, *"Now it came to pass after these things that God tested Abraham, and said to him, 'Abraham!' And he said, 'Here I am.'"* I am not talking about the kind of testing where God would hold your hand to a hot stovetop and see how long you can endure it. No good father would ever do that to their child. I'm talking about the type of testing that prepares you and strengthens you for the plan and purpose He has for you.

I remember my dad making my brother and I do chores every day after school. I say make because we didn't want to do them. We could either pick up the dog poop, or we could vacuum the living room. My dad also had me paint the gutter on our roof in our backyard. It was a random color that didn't match our house, yet I climbed up on the ladder and did it anyway. I also remember my dad giving me a $100 bill to go get dinner for the family from the local Taco Bell. I brought him back the $83 and some change, and this is what he said to me, "Daniel, do you know why I gave you the $100 and not your brothers? Because I could trust you to bring me all the change back." My dad tested me. He tested me by seeing if I would listen to him and do my chores. He tested me to see if I would be a man of integrity and bring him the large sum of money back. He tested me to see if I would do what he asked, even if it was to paint our gutter an odd color. Even though I didn't have a close relationship with him growing up, I simply listened to him because he was my dad. The tests my dad put me through have allowed me to be a good steward of the gifts God has given me today. What God put in me as a child, He used testing to refine it and bring it to the forefront of my character. I benefit today because of it.

God tested Joseph as well. Joseph was second in command. He had been hurt by his brothers. Could you imagine how he would have treated his brothers if he wasn't humbled through the hardship he went through? He would have had all of them killed! Then how would God's promise be preserved? How would the Savior come? Joseph went through what he went through so he could respond to his brothers appropriately. God needed him to respond in love. So, God used the hardships in his life to humble him and mold him. He tested him to see if he would be faithful. To see if he would listen. To see if he would give up or not (Deuteronomy 8:2).

I'm not saying that God incited Potiphar's wife to attempt to commit adultery with Joseph. That goes against the doctrine of Scripture in James 1:12–16. Please take a moment to read it in your Bible. I'm not even saying that God incited Joseph's brothers to want to kill him and sell him. You can clearly see from that story that it was the brother's own jealousy that plotted against Joseph. His brother Reuben was looking out for himself. He was trying to cover up the poor decision he made, which was sleeping with his dad's concubine. He came up with the idea to sell Joseph and not kill him. But he didn't propose that because he cared for Joseph. He told the brothers to put Joseph in a pit so that they would leave him alone, and then he could come back and save Joseph and take him to his father, Jacob. Then he would be on his father's good side again. But his brothers sold him into Egypt before Reuben returned. This shows me that mankind can do bad all by themselves and that not every trial in our life comes from God.

But God certainly didn't stop any of these things from happening because He knew where He was taking Joseph. He knew where Joseph would ultimately end up. God allows a lot of things to happen to us because we need to be prepared for the responsibility ahead of us. We have to remember that this life is not our final destination. While suffering is not fun, it's not forever. Many hard things will come against us simply because we live in a fallen world. But there are times where God will initiate hardship in our lives. I will talk about this more in the next chapter. But we have to know that God is always for us. Even when He tests us, by allowing or initiating, He is faithful and good.

A Good Life

We can sum up Genesis 45–49 from a New Testament reference by Stephen in the Book of Acts. Please take a moment to read in your Bible Acts 7:9–16. Joseph died at 110 years old at the end of Genesis 50. Even though he died, his life was not lived in vain. Everything he went through was for God and others. He still lived a blessed life in the process; he was married, had two sons, got to see three generations of his grandkids, saw his father, reconciled with his brothers, became vice president over the entire world, and ultimately kept his faith in God. The blessings outweigh the hardships! But the hardships were part of the process. And both blessings and hardships will be involved in the lives of those who are sent by God. When we understand the bigger purpose at hand, we will gladly give our lives over to God, and we will gladly endure whatever comes before us. Because we know that what we are going through is for the glory of God and for the benefit of others. We go through hell on earth to give others a chance, to not go through hell for eternity.

A true Jesus follower is sent by God so others can be saved!

CHAPTER NINE
GOD IS GOOD

A true Jesus follower knows God is good no matter what!

Just before Joseph died, he had a conversation with his brothers. Their father Jacob passed away, and now the brothers are afraid that Joseph is going to finally take vengeance on them. Joseph does not respond in such a way. He responds in humility and blesses his brothers. But Joseph says something towards the end of his life that many in the church today quote often. Joseph says, "But as for you, you meant evil against me, but God meant it for good." Joseph knew that God was good no matter what he went through in his life. Let's look at this final moment of Joseph's life so that we, too, can say the same as him; God is good no matter what!

> *When Joseph's brothers saw that their father was dead, they said, 'Perhaps Joseph will hate us, and may actually repay us for all the evil which we did to him.' So they sent messengers to Joseph, saying, 'Before your father died he commanded, saying, 'Thus you shall say to Joseph: 'I beg you, please forgive the trespass of your brothers and their sin; for they did evil to you.' Now, please, forgive the trespass of the servants of the God of*

your father.' And Joseph wept when they spoke to him. Then his brothers also went and fell down before his face, and they said, 'Behold, we are your servants.' Joseph said to them, 'Do not be afraid, for am I in the place of God? But as for you, you meant evil against me; but God meant it for good, in order to bring it about as it is this day, to save many people alive. Now therefore, do not be afraid; I will provide for you and your little ones.' And he comforted them and spoke kindly to them.

Genesis 50:15–21

It's Not God's Fault

I was following Jesus for about two and a half years when I encountered a conversation with my brother's friend. We began to talk about faith in God, and she proceeded to tell me why she doesn't believe in God. She believed in His existence, but she didn't believe in His character. She told me how her grandmother was sick. She and the family began to pray for the grandma, but she died the next day. Her question to me was, "If God was so good, then why didn't He spare my grandmother?" She let a tragedy determine her relationship with God.

Then the Lord God took the man and put him in the garden of Eden to tend and keep it. And the Lord God commanded the man, saying, 'Of every tree of the garden you may freely eat; but of the tree of the knowledge of good and evil you shall not eat, for in the day that you eat of it you shall surely die.'

Genesis 2:15–17

Death: both physical and spiritual, has now entered the picture. Now this body that God gave us will not go on forever in this world. One day we will get a new glorified body according to 1 Corinthians 15. But we have to physically die first before that happens. Genesis 2:7 and Ecclesiastes 12:7 tell us that our body will go back to the earth just as it came and that our spirit will go back to God, who gave it to us in the first place. Hebrews 9:27 says, *"And as it is appointed for men to die once, but after this the judgment."* So, the scary part of death is that our spirit will live on, either with God or without God. We will either be with God in heaven or away from Him in hell (Revelation 20–22). Wherever we go, our spirit will live on for eternity!

Romans 5:12 continues to bring clarity on death by saying, *"Therefore, just as through one man sin entered the world, and death through sin, and thus death spread to all men, because all sinned."* How did death come into the world? Through sin. Who sinned? Humans did. So, who is to blame for death in our world? We are. Death is not God's fault; it's ours. God is so good because instead of leaving us in death (both physically and spiritually), He died as a direct result of the death that we caused. We messed up, and yet God cleaned up our mess. The fact that God would die on behalf of the death that we caused shows that He is a good God no matter what happens to us in our lifetime.

God never promised us that He would stop every person from dying before we wanted them to die. God promised us that death would enter through our sin. Sin caused death, not God. So, we can't blame God for something that He never promised wouldn't happen. Can God intervene and save people's lives? Of course. I have seen it happen! But foundationally, He made a way for everyone who chooses to believe in Him and His Gospel to be with Him and not be away from Him for eternity. That's a good God to me! From the beginning, God said, "When you sin, you will die." And all have sinned; therefore, we all will die (Romans 3:23). But Jesus is our hope, and when we trust God's good plan of salvation for our lives, we no longer need to fear; rather, we can rest in His great love towards us (Romans 5:8).

Don't Let Death Do Us Part

The three main causes for death that I see in the Bible are sin, Satan, and sovereignty. I already explained how sin causes death. After the fall in Genesis 3, you see in the very next chapter of Genesis 4, where Cain kills his brother Abel. Why? Because of jealousy, which is sin. Then you see that Satan does get permission from God in the Book of Revelation to kill some of His saints (Revelation 13:7). You also see that Satan entered the heart of Judas, who betrayed Jesus and then ultimately had Him killed. You also see from 2 Samuel 12 and Joshua 7 where David and Achan sinned, and it caused death in their lives. David's sin with Bathsheba caused their first child to die. Achan's sin caused his entire family, including himself, to die. So not only does the sinful nature of the world cause death, but individual peoples' sin can cause death too. And yes, the enemy, with God's permission only, can cause death (Job 2:6). But how should you respond when God, out of His sovereignty, chooses to take back the life that He gave?

We have already discussed the foundation of how God owes us nothing because, as humans, we have sinned. Not only that, but we are human, and He is the only God. He can do whatever He wants, and He doesn't have to check in with anybody (Psalm 115:3). So, who are we to ask God anything in the first place? (Romans 9:20). Yet God is good and desires a close relationship with us. He gives us insight into Himself from His Word. God doesn't hide anything about Himself in His Word. He puts it all out there so that we can see clearly who He is. If God wasn't good, then wouldn't He hide things from us? If He didn't want us to know something or if He was just stringing us along, then couldn't He easily hide things from us about Himself? Instead, He chose to speak freely to us and tell us who He is. He wants us to know Him fully, and He wants us to choose Him with all our hearts. Even if in His sovereignty, He chooses to take the life that He gave in the first place.

The reason I am writing about death and God's goodness is because when I talk to people about God's love, the major factor of why people walk away from God is that they struggle to understand death. They let death separate them from God. But God didn't let death separate Him from us. He didn't let our death get in the way of His love for us. So why do we let death get in the way of our love for Him? I remember reading stories in the Bible, like in Ezekiel 24, where Ezekiel is met by God with a difficult instruction. These stories were difficult for me to wrap my head around them. In Ezekiel 24, Ezekiel's life is physically impacted for the sake of the spiritual truth that God is about to speak to Israel. Please take a moment to read Ezekiel 24:15–27 in your Bible.

Who took away Ezekiel's wife? God did. But why? As a serious sign to Israel because of their horrible disobedience towards God. But that's not fair for Ezekiel. What's not fair about it? That God gave him life, gave him a wife, and then took his wife when He needed her to be taken? God is God, so who are we as men to say anything? Job 1:21 says, "And he said: 'Naked I came from my mother's womb, And naked shall I return there. The Lord gave, and the Lord has taken away; Blessed be the name of the Lord.'" We sing it, but do we really believe it? Ezekiel's wife didn't die as a direct result of his individual sin nor of Satan. You could argue that it was because of Israel's sin. Yet, I also see a truth here that God, in His sovereignty, chose to take what He originally gave. As God, He has every right to do that. Instead of hiding this truth from us, He tells us plainly. This, too, is why God is good no matter what!

Worship God in Spirit and Truth

I wrote about the tragedy of my first son in my first book, but I still remember yelling at God when my first son died. Following Jesus since February 4, 2011, and having my son die on September 8, 2018, I knew God long enough to know that nothing passes through His hands without His permission. I took a moment alone in my house and went at it with God. I began to cry, scream and yell at Him, "You took him. You took my son. You can call it whatever You want, sin, sovereignty, or Satan. In the end, You took my son." I was beside myself. Then the Holy Spirit began to graciously minister to me, and He showed me a picture of God with tears in His eyes. He was pointing off to the side and sort of behind Him, implying that the direction He was pointing in was indicating that my son was there. He showed me that God clearly has Him in His presence. Then the Lord asked me, "And even if I did take your son, will you still worship Me?" Before I could even answer, the Lord said, "Because if you answer Me anything other than yes, you will still worship Me, then you don't really love Me for who I am, but for what I can give you." I began to weep uncontrollably as I repented and told God I was sorry.

I was so hurt, and I felt like the only person that I could ever depend on was God. But when my son was taken from me and when I thought God did it, it was hard for me to go to God. One of my mentors told me, "Daniel, you need to go to the One who has him." But my response back was, "How can I go to the One who took him." That's what led me to my upsetting moment with God. Then I heard gently in my spirit, "By the way, I didn't take him." To this day, I don't know if the death of my first child was a result of sin, the fall, my individual sin, Satan, or God's sovereignty. The last thing I heard from God on the matter would imply that it wasn't Him. The conclusion I came to was that we live in a fallen world, and Christ followers are not immune to the curse of the land. The curse is not removed off the land until the new heaven and new earth (Revelation 22:3). Death no longer has a spiritual hold on us, but we still reap the consequences of the pangs of physical death in this world. Whether it's our child or our grandmother, death is part of our fallen world. But death is not easy, nor is it meant to be taken lightly. I think about my son Joseph every day. If it was up to me, I would want him here with me right now. But the question God asked me taught me a valuable lesson, "Would I still worship Him even if He did take my son?" I would, and I am. I am still walking with Jesus wholeheartedly today.

What About You?

A close friend of mine began to struggle in their faith once hardship hit their life. They didn't expect it, and they didn't know how to handle it. This is what they said to me one day, "The real reason I walked away from God is because I want a family. I don't want to live in fear of God deciding to test my faith by taking that away from me and having to press into Him, so He can heal the pain He caused and deepen my relationship with Him. That's what we call a toxic relationship."

If this is the condition of your heart, then you are missing the point. I wouldn't have my life, my wife, or my children if it wasn't for God. In the beginning, there was God. Everything that was made was made through Him. God is first and always will be! The first and great commandment says to love the LORD your God with all your heart, soul, mind, and strength (Matthew 22:37). The LORD is the One who saved us and therefore said not to have any other gods before Him (Exodus 20:1–3). God is not opposed to giving these things to us. He wants to give us good things! Matthew 6:32–33 says, *"For after all these things the Gentiles seek. For your heavenly Father knows that you need all these things. But seek first the kingdom of God and His righteousness, and all these things shall be added to you."*

When I put God first, He began to add to my life. He gave me my wife. *"He who finds a wife finds a good thing, and obtains favor from the Lord"* (Proverbs 18:22). God gave me my children. *"Behold, children are a heritage from the Lord, the fruit of the womb is a reward"* (Psalm 127:3). God gave me my life. *"And the Lord God formed man of the dust of the ground, and breathed into his nostrils the breath of life; and man became a living being"* (Genesis 2:7). Even Jesus shares a sobering truth in Luke 14:26 by saying, *"If anyone comes to Me and does not hate his father and mother, wife and children, brothers and sisters, yes, and his own life also, he cannot be My disciple."* God doesn't want us to despise our families; He gave them to us. But He does want us to choose Him first! As my pastor always says, "God first. Life second." The creature can never come before the Creator (Romans 1:25). That was the problem with Israel in the Ezekiel story I shared above. They chose the temple of God over the presence of God. They neglected their Savior.

Ask yourself these questions: Is God good in your eyes simply because of who He is? Or is God only good in your eyes when you get what you want? You need to settle the truth in your heart that God is good no matter what. Because there are many more passages in the Bible that reveal that God has every right in His sovereignty to do what He wants to do. Look at this connection between the theology with Moses and the blind man in the gospel of John:

> *Then Moses said to the Lord, 'O my Lord, I am not eloquent, neither before nor since You have spoken to Your servant; but I am slow of speech and slow of tongue.' So the Lord said to him, 'Who has made man's mouth? Or who makes the mute, the deaf, the seeing, or the blind? Have not I, the Lord?'*

> **Exodus 4:10-11**

> *Now as Jesus passed by, He saw a man who was blind from birth. And His disciples asked Him, saying, 'Rabbi, who sinned, this man or his*

parents, that he was born blind?' Jesus answered,
'Neither this man nor his parents sinned, but that
the works of God should be revealed in him.'

John 9:1–4

Bible verses like these can make a new believer stumble. But I see it that God isn't hiding anything from us, and by revealing the truth about His sovereignty and the truth of death, that deems Him good for not hiding His truth from us. God also doesn't owe me anything, and on behalf of my mistakes, He still gave me His Son Jesus. Not only did He give me Jesus, but He gave me a second son after my son Joseph. God gave me my son Elisha when He didn't have to.

His Hands

I've included another picture at the end of this chapter that I drew. I drew this picture from an encounter/vision I received from the Holy Spirit. Acts 2:17 says, *"'And it shall come to pass in the last days, says God, that I will pour out of My Spirit on all flesh; your sons and your daughters shall prophesy, your young men shall see visions, our old men shall dream dreams."* It was a few months after my son had passed, and the Lord took me into an encounter with Him. I was awake when this happened, so that constitutes a vision. A dream obviously happens when you are asleep. In this vision, the Lord showed me my son Joseph being in heaven. Jesus told me, "Give Me your pain; I can take it!" I was struggling to do so. But in the vision, the Lord said, "Put out your hands." So, I did. Then Jesus put His hands over my hands, and when He slid his hands away from mine, my son's hands were in my hands. It was a beautiful moment, and I began to weep uncontrollably. I went home and told my wife this vision, and once again, the Holy Spirit prompted me to draw this picture for her. So, I did. I drew this picture on December 24, 2018. I've titled it: *His Hands.* What Jesus showed me was especially meaningful because my wife and I were not able to obtain our son's handprints in the hospital. The nurse could only get a clear print of his feet.

The hands with the nails in the wrists represent Jesus. Since He lived, died, and rose again, my son lives! One day, my wife and I will see Jesus and our Joseph again! The little hands inside represent my son's hands. The hands in the middle are my wife's hands. At the bottom are my hands gently guiding my wife's hands towards Jesus. Notice there is no darkness in the middle of this drawing as it represents where Jesus and my son Joseph reside (in heaven). We have hope for a new life where there are no more sickness, death, pain, or tears (Revelation 21:4)! The darkness represents the fallen state of this world. As I already discussed, we are not always immune to sin in this world. But in the midst of the darkness, there is light! Just like Joseph in the story of Genesis, evil will come against us. But God truly takes all evil situations, including the severe truth of death, and makes it good.

A true Jesus follower knows God is good no matter what!

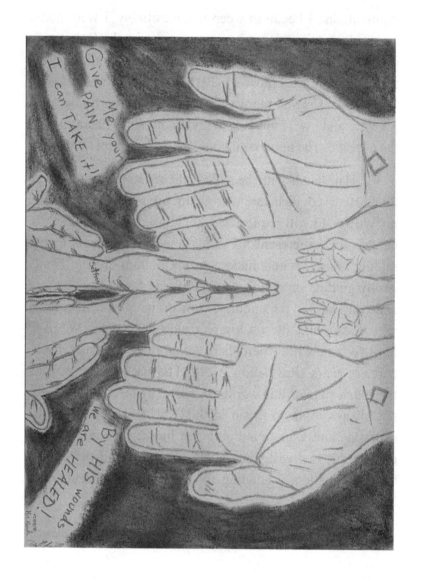

CONCLUSION

Texas Trips

I want to conclude this book with a final story. In April of 2013, I was driving through Texas for a college basketball tournament that I was about to play in Joplin, Missouri. At that time, I was a youth leader at my church, and I had been serving the youth for just shy of one year. There was talk about me taking over the high school portion of the group, while our youth pastor would focus on the middle school group and oversee the entire program. My pastor was reaching out to me while I was on this trip. He wanted me to decide. But I was more focused on the basketball tournament ahead. I told him I would think about it. Then he responded back, "Don't let the devil put fear in you, for what you know God has called you to do." That was convicting. Towards the end of the basketball tournament, God opened my eyes to the truth behind my pastor's text message to me, and I made the decision to become the high school youth director. About a week later, I ended up becoming the youth pastor of the church, and I oversaw the entire youth program. Our youth pastor at the time stepped down, and God called me up to bat. It was His will for my life.

In September of 2019, I went back to Texas for a leaders' conference at a significantly large church in Dallas. As soon as we got in the state, I began to think about that initial decision I made to say yes to being the youth pastor of our church. About six years had passed since then, and

I experienced all sorts of hardship. I experienced hardship for a few reasons, but it was mainly because I was young in my faith walk, young as a person, and inexperienced in leadership and team management. Also, internal turmoil from things in my past life started to rear its ugly head. A lot came against me in such a short amount of time, and on this Dallas trip in 2019, I was still in the middle of severe turmoil. My wife was pregnant for the second time while I was on this trip. She was twenty-five weeks pregnant, which was the same age as our first son when he died in the womb. I was contending with God to hold my son because I had already gone through so much hardship in those first six years of ministry. I didn't know how much more I could take. God blessed me with my son Elisha. It helped me to keep moving forward in my faith in Jesus.

In September of 2021, I went back to that leadership conference in Texas, and the Holy Spirit began to minister to me again. The Holy Spirit began to show me an overview of my life. He showed me when I was a child, the elementary school I went to, my friendships, my neighborhood, and my family. Then He said, "I picked you! Out of everyone that I could pick, I picked you." This quiet, shy, and gentle kid from Folsom, California. Then He told me, "The One who matters most (referring to Himself) has picked you. But also, your wife has picked you. Your sons have picked you. Your twin brother has picked you. Your friend Josiah has picked you. All this affirms My choosing of you." Let this truth resonate with you as well. God has chosen you!

Then He began to minister to me about the nation of Israel. Reminding me about how these people were so close to God. His presence was manifested right in front of their eyes. He spoke to them from Mount Sinai. They saw His signs and wonders in Egypt. He provided food and water in the desert for them. He delivered them from their slavery. Yet, they didn't think it was worth it. Why did they have to obey God when the rest of the world could do whatever they wanted? They tested Him ten times in their desert journey. They doubted Him and denied Him ten times. He said, "Don't be like that. Don't doubt the plan that I have for your life." We can learn from the Old Testament. If we were still bound to the Old Testament living, then I, too, would have failed in this walk with God, and I would not have made it to the promised land that God has for my life. I'm grateful that we are in the New Testament. But I don't want to take His grace for granted either.

Then He showed me Joshua and how he and Israel defeated thirty-one kings. How there are obvious battles we must face as we walk with God. He showed me how even though Israel disobeyed God and ended up being wiped out as a nation, that He had mercy on them and restored them as a nation in 1948. This has never been done by any other nation. God showed me how Israel still flourishes today and how He continues to protect them and provide for them. Then He showed me the New Jerusalem from the Book of Revelation and how Israel will forever be with Him in the New Heaven and New Earth for all eternity. He showed me the clear path that He had for my life, and He showed me the enemy standing off at a distance, yelling at me and trying to get me off track. God said, "Stop listening to the enemy." I need to let God's Word be the truth and the lamp unto my feet and the light unto my path.

The Lord sealed this ministry time by telling me that just like Israel, He has an eternal plan for my life as well. I will be blessed in this life now and into eternity. What He has called me to, He promises to take me the distance. This applies to you as well. Because we are grafted into His family and grand plan. God showed me His faithfulness! Once I said yes to believe in Him, follow Him and fulfill the God dream that He put in my heart, all hell began to break loose towards me. Hell sent every agent possible my way to get me to quit. For some reason, the enemy can see what we can't. He has been doing this a lot longer than us, and he has studied mankind enough. But nothing can thwart God's plan for our lives (Philippians 1:6)!

God showed me the milestones of each Texas Trip, and even though I went through extreme hardships; dealing with past hurts, division with other Christ followers, ministry failures, physical fights to defend my family, arguments with family lasting years, death of my firstborn son, my wife almost dying on two different occasions, hardships in marriage, constant spiritual attacks from the enemy and so much more. Yet, God is faithful and has brought me this far and will continue to bring me through whatever comes my way (2 Thessalonians 3:3). This truth is for you too! Because it's all about Him and pointing people to Him anyway! Israel was meant to be an example to the world around them. The world would look at their lives and wonder how they are so blessed and how they endure hardship so joyously. They could then point people to the LORD and say, "It's all Him!" I want my life to do the same thing. I want people to look at me and see Jesus. If you want the same thing, then follow Him until the end. Don't give up. Don't quit. As I once heard someone say, "You got this because God has got you!"

Now I Know

When I think back to sitting on that mattress and hearing God speak Romans 8:28 to me through a Scrubs TV Show, I can say with full confidence that His Word is true. God truly works all things together for good. But I am thankful that He revealed to me the next verse, Romans 8:29. I know that I will live a blessed life here on earth. I know that this faith walk will require a testing of my faith. I also know that it will require that I endure hardship. I know that I will be made more into the image of Jesus. This helps people see God in me, which then points people to Him. Jesus is the person we originally looked like in the first place. Not in His physical appearance, but rather His character. I know that God will even use hardships to mold me back into my original image. God did so to Jesus. Since I follow Jesus, I can expect the same treatment.

In writing this book, my hope is that you believe that God is good and faithful towards you. His plan is to prosper you and carry you all the way into eternity with Him. I wrote this book so that you wouldn't be blindsided by trials and opposition. These are things that no one told me about when I gave my life to Jesus. I was very much uninformed about what a true follower of Jesus really looked like. I truly thought that after I gave my life to Jesus, that I would never be tempted to sin again. I truly thought that after I gave my life to Jesus, that I would never go through anything hard again. Both of those misconceptions couldn't have been further from the truth. I said to the LORD, "If I have the opportunity to write a book that will inform people of your goodness and faithfulness in the midst of the trials of following Jesus, then please help me do it." I'm thankful to Jesus that He has blessed my hands in this work and gifted me for such a project as this. I truly hope and pray that you are encouraged to follow Jesus with all your heart. I pray that as you have seen the life of Joseph in Genesis and how our lives parallel his, you will be strengthened and filled with new hope. Regardless of what comes your way in this faith walk, Jesus will see to it that you will make it with Him to the very end. Now go and live the Unshakeable life of a true Jesus follower! God bless you.

But now that Timothy has come to us from you, and brought us good news of your faith and love, and that you always have good remembrance of us, greatly desiring to see us, as we also to see you— therefore, brethren, in all our affliction and distress we were comforted concerning you by your faith. For now we live, if you stand fast in the Lord.

1 Thessalonians 3:6–8

Only knowing the blessings makes you breakable but having awareness of afflictions makes you unshakeable!

PERSONAL REFLECTION OR SMALL GROUP QUESTIONS

Here is a compilation of questions derived from each chapter in this book. You can choose to answer them personally or in a small group. If you choose to answer them personally, then I would encourage you to get a journal and take the adequate time to reflect on each question. Don't rush the journaling process. Take the time to let the Holy Spirit speak to you. You can answer the questions after you read each chapter, each section, or you can read the entire book and answer the questions afterward. If you choose to answer these questions in a group setting, then I would encourage you to have your group members read the book also so that they understand the whole story. You can answer the questions from each chapter at your own pace. You can determine how many weeks you want to get together and discuss these questions. Do whatever works for your group. Let the Holy Spirit lead you through.

Chapter One:

- What does your family background look like?
- How has God provided for you throughout your life?
- Are you letting God or your family history define you?

Chapter Two:

- What's your calling?
- Are you living out your calling now?
- What opposition have you experienced because of your calling?

Chapter Three:

- What have you had to give up to fulfill your God dream?
- What are you still holding onto that you were supposed to let go of?
- Is what you are holding on to worth not completing what God is asking you to do?

Chapter Four:

- What tangible evidence of God's presence have you experienced?
- Have you been water baptized?
- Have you experienced the outpouring/infilling of the Holy Spirit in your life?

Chapter Five:

- Where are you at when it comes to sexual sin? Are you looking at pornography? Are you masturbating? Are you committing adultery? Are you having sex outside of marriage? Are you struggling with same-sex attraction?
- Do you want God's help? Do you want to flee from sexual sin?

Chapter Six:

- Have you ever experienced a spiritual gift?
- What are your spiritual gifts?

Chapter Seven:

- Do you relate more to the Pharisee sitting at the table or the woman lying on the floor?

- Is there anyone in your life that you need to restore your relationship with?

Chapter Eight:

- Are you willing to be sent by God so others can be saved?
- In these one hundred years of life, what could be more valuable to us than living with God for eternity?
- Has God ever tested you? What is the difference between testing and tempting?

Chapter Nine:

- Have you ever blamed God?
- Is God good in your eyes simply because of who He is? Or is God only good in your eyes when you get what you want?
- What do you think about the tough passages of Scripture that were shared?

Introduction/Conclusion:

- What stood out to you the most at the beginning and end of this book?

ABOUT THE AUTHOR

Pastor Daniel Aguilar is the associate pastor at East River Fellowship in Hillsboro, Oregon. He has attended this church since August 2012. His ministry focus has been youth, young adults, men's ministry, and evangelism. Daniel graduated from Multnomah University with a bachelor's degree in Bible and theology and pastoral ministry. He is married to Sonja Aguilar, who graduated from Pacific University and is a dual-language kindergarten teacher. They have two sons, Joseph, who is in heaven, and Elisha. Daniel enjoys basketball, wrestling with his son, art, coffee, and walks with his wife. Daniel is also the author of *The Weapons of our Warfare: Living Victoriously in Jesus Christ.*

ENDNOTES

1. Throughout the book, you will notice Scripture references in parentheses, in the middle, or at the end of some sentences. The reason for this is I want the reader to know where my thoughts are coming from. They are coming from the Bible. They are not my own thoughts. You don't have to stop reading this book and read every Scripture that is referenced. There will be times where I will ask the reader to do so, but it will be evident which Scriptures to stop and read.

2. Conformed: σύμμορφος, ον, of the same shape as. Liddell, H. G., Scott, R., Jones, H. S., and McKenzie, R. (1996). A Greek-English lexicon (p. 1680). Oxford: Clarendon Press. σύμμορφος (symmorphos), ον (on): similar in form, pertaining to being conformed, to being like. Swanson, J. (1997). Dictionary of Biblical Languages with Semantic Domains: Greek (New Testament) (electronic ed.). Oak Harbor: Logos Research Systems, Inc.

3. Quoted from a friend. Context comes from Matthew 3 and 4.

4. Repent: μετανοέω (metanoeō). vb. to repent, change one's mind. In the NT, generally refers not simply to changing one's mind but to turning back to God. The original meaning of metanoeō is "to change one's mind." DiFransico, L. (2014). Repentance. D. Mangum, D. R. Brown, R. Klippenstein, & R. Hurst (Eds.), Lexham Theological Wordbook. Bellingham, WA: Lexham Press.

5. Baptize: βαπτίζω (baptizō). vb. to immerse. Expresses the action of immersing something or someone into liquid (usually water). Snyder, B. J. (2014). Baptism. D. Mangum, D. R. Brown, R. Klippenstein, & R. Hurst (Eds.), Lexham Theological Wordbook. Bellingham, WA: Lexham Press.

6. Regeneration: πἄλιγγενεσία, ἡ, rebirth, regeneration. Liddell, H. G., Scott, R., Jones, H. S., & McKenzie, R. (1996). A Greek-English lexicon (p. 1291). Oxford: Clarendon Press.

7. Renewal: 364 ἀνακαίνωσις (anakainōsis). Swanson, J. (1997). Dictionary of Biblical Languages with Semantic Domains: Greek (New Testament) (electronic ed.). Oak Harbor: Logos Research Systems, Inc.

8. Sin: ἁμαρτάνω (hamartanō): vb.;sin, do wrong, i.e., to act or intend contrary to the will and law of God. Swanson, J. (1997).

Dictionary of Biblical Languages with Semantic Domains: Greek (New Testament) (electronic ed.). Oak Harbor: Logos Research Systems, Inc.

9. I also need to give credit to pastor Jerry Dirman of The Rock Church in Anaheim, California. Through his program Operation Solid Lives, level 4 of their discipleship program, they provided some of the definitions that are listed.

10. Pastor Ben Dixon is the lead pastor at Northwest Church in Federal Way, Washington. He has written two books, Prophesy and Hearing God, that are very helpful in the pursuit of what their titles suggest.

11. My first book, The Weapons of Our Warfare: Living Victoriously in Jesus Christ, will provide you with a more holistic understanding of some of the stories shared in this book. While the topics of both my books are different, they do build off one another when it comes to my life story and revealing more of the character of God. You can purchase my first book on Amazon.com.

12. Scott McNamara is an evangelist and founder of Jesus at the Door. He is Director of Evangelism at Nations Church Orlando. He is also a ministry partner with my church, East River Fellowship. He published the book Jesus at the Door: Evangelism Made Easy. He has a YouTube channel if you want to check out his approach.

13. Reconcile: change a person from enmity to friendship, reconcile σφέας. Liddell, H. G., Scott, R., Jones, H. S., & McKenzie, R. (1996). A Greek-English lexicon (p. 899). Oxford: Clarendon Press.

14. Righteousness: be put right with, be in a right relationship with. Swanson, J. (1997). Dictionary of Biblical Languages with Semantic Domains: Greek (New Testament) (electronic ed.). Oak Harbor: Logos Research Systems, Inc.

CPSIA information can be obtained
at www.ICGtesting.com
Printed in the USA
FSHW010658080222